Lecture Notes in Computer Science   12990

More information about this subseries at https://link.springer.com/bookseries/7409

Liang-Jie Zhang (Ed.)

Edge Computing – EDGE 2021

5th International Conference
Held as Part of the Services Conference Federation, SCF 2021
Virtual Event, December 10–14, 2021
Proceedings

 Springer

Editor
Liang-Jie Zhang 🆔
Kingdee International Software Group Co., Ltd.
Shenzhen, China

ISSN 0302-9743 ISSN 1611-3349 (electronic)
Lecture Notes in Computer Science
ISBN 978-3-030-96503-7 ISBN 978-3-030-96504-4 (eBook)
https://doi.org/10.1007/978-3-030-96504-4

LNCS Sublibrary: SL3 – Information Systems and Applications, incl. Internet/Web, and HCI

This Springer imprint is published by the registered company Springer Nature Switzerland AG
The registered company address is: Gewerbestrasse 11, 6330 Cham, Switzerland

Preface

The International Conference on Edge Computing (EDGE) aims to become a prime international forum for both researchers and industry practitioners to exchange the latest fundamental advances in the state of the art and practice of edge computing, identify emerging research topics, and define the future of edge computing.

EDGE is a member of Services Conference Federation (SCF). SCF 2021 comprised the following 10 collocated service-oriented sister conferences: the International Conference on Web Services (ICWS 2021), the International Conference on Cloud Computing (CLOUD 2021), the International Conference on Services Computing (SCC 2021), the International Conference on Big Data (BigData 2021), the International Conference on AI and Mobile Services (AIMS 2021), the World Congress on Services (SERVICES 2021), the International Conference on Internet of Things (ICIOT 2021), the International Conference on Cognitive Computing (ICCC 2021), the International Conference on Edge Computing (EDGE 2021), and the International Conference on Blockchain (ICBC 2021).

This volume presents the accepted papers for EDGE 2021, held virtually over the Internet during December 10–14, 2021. EDGE 2021 put its focus on the state of the art and practice of edge computing, which covered localized resource sharing and connections with the cloud. We accepted seven papers for the proceedings. Each paper was reviewed by at least three independent members of the EDGE 2021 Program Committee. We are pleased to thank the authors whose submissions and participation made this conference possible. We also want to express our thanks to the Organizing Committee and Program Committee members for their dedication in helping to organize the conference and reviewing the submissions. We look forward to your future contributions as volunteers, authors, and conference participants in the fast-growing worldwide services innovations community.

December 2021   Liang-Jie Zhang

Organization

EDGE 2021 General Chair

Ling Geng   F5 Networks, USA

EDGE 2021 Program Chair

Liang-Jie Zhang   Kingdee International Software Group Co., Ltd., China

Services Conference Federation (SCF 2021)

General Chairs

Wu Chou   Essenlix Corporation, USA
Calton Pu (Co-chair)   Georgia Tech, USA
Dimitrios Georgakopoulos   Swinburne University of Technology, Australia

Program Chairs

Liang-Jie Zhang   Kingdee International Software Group Co., Ltd., China
Ali Arsanjani   Amazon Web Services, USA

CFO

Min Luo   Georgia Tech, USA

Industry Track Chairs

Awel Dico   Etihad Airways, UAE
Rajesh Subramanyan   Amazon Web Services, USA
Siva Kantamneni   Deloitte Consulting, USA

Industry Exhibit and International Affairs Chair

Zhixiong Chen   Mercy College, USA

Operations Committee

Jing Zeng	China Gridcom Co., Ltd., China
Yishuang Ning	Tsinghua University, China
Sheng He	Tsinghua University, China

Steering Committee

Calton Pu (Co-chair)	Georgia Tech, USA
Liang-Jie Zhang (Co-chair)	Kingdee International Software Group Co., Ltd., China

EDGE 2021 Program Committee

Tao Han	New Jersey Institute of Technology, USA
Tessema Mengistu	George Mason University, USA
Rui André Oliveira	University of Lisbon, Portugal
Arun Ravindran	University of North Carolina at Charlotte, USA
Midori Sugaya	Shibaura Institute of Technology, Japan
Javid Taheri	Karlstad University, Sweden
Hung-Yu Wei	National Taiwan University, Taiwan
Mengjun Xie	University of Tennessee at Chattanooga, USA
Jing Zeng	China Gridcom Co., Ltd., China

Conference Sponsor – Services Society

The Services Society (S2) is a non-profit professional organization that has been created to promote worldwide research and technical collaboration in services innovations among academia and industrial professionals. Its members are volunteers from industry and academia with common interests. S2 is registered in the USA as a "501(c) organization", which means that it is an American tax-exempt non-profit organization. S2 collaborates with other professional organizations to sponsor or co-sponsor conferences and to promote an effective services curriculum in colleges and universities. S2 initiates and promotes a "Services University" program worldwide to bridge the gap between industrial needs and university instruction.

The services sector accounted for 79.5% of the GDP of the USA in 2016. Hong Kong has one of the world's most service-oriented economies, with the services sector accounting for more than 90% of GDP. As such, the Services Society has formed 10 Special Interest Groups (SIGs) to support technology and domain specific professional activities:

- Special Interest Group on Web Services (SIG-WS)
- Special Interest Group on Services Computing (SIG-SC)
- Special Interest Group on Services Industry (SIG-SI)
- Special Interest Group on Big Data (SIG-BD)
- Special Interest Group on Cloud Computing (SIG-CLOUD)
- Special Interest Group on Artificial Intelligence (SIG-AI)
- Special Interest Group on Edge Computing (SIG-EC)
- Special Interest Group on Cognitive Computing (SIG-CC)
- Special Interest Group on Blockchain (SIG-BC)
- Special Interest Group on Internet of Things (SIG-IOT)

About the Services Conference Federation (SCF)

As the founding member of the Services Conference Federation (SCF), the First International Conference on Web Services (ICWS) was held in June 2003 in Las Vegas, USA. A sister event, the First International Conference on Web Services - Europe 2003 (ICWS-Europe 2003) was held in Germany in October of the same year. In 2004, ICWS-Europe was changed to the European Conference on Web Services (ECOWS), which was held in Erfurt, Germany. The 19th edition in the conference series, SCF 2021, was held virtually over the Internet during December 10–14, 2021.

In the past 18 years, the ICWS community has expanded from Web engineering innovations to scientific research for the whole services industry. The service delivery platforms have expanded to mobile platforms, the Internet of Things (IoT), cloud computing, and edge computing. The services ecosystem has gradually been enabled, value added, and intelligence embedded through enabling technologies such as big data, artificial intelligence, and cognitive computing. In the coming years, transactions with multiple parties involved will be transformed by blockchain.

Based on the technology trends and best practices in the field, SCF will continue serving as the conference umbrella's code name for all services-related conferences. SCF 2021 defined the future of the New ABCDE (AI, Blockchain, Cloud, big Data, Everything is connected), which enable IOT and support the "5G for Services Era". SCF 2021 featured 10 colocated conferences all centered around the topic of "services", each focusing on exploring different themes (e.g. web-based services, cloud-based services, big data-based services, services innovation lifecycle, AI-driven ubiquitous services, blockchain-driven trust service-ecosystems, industry-specific services and applications, and emerging service-oriented technologies). The SCF 2021 members were as follows:

1. The 2021 International Conference on Web Services (ICWS 2021, http://icws.org/), which was the flagship conference for web-based services featuring web services modeling, development, publishing, discovery, composition, testing, adaptation, and delivery, as well as the latest API standards.
2. The 2021 International Conference on Cloud Computing (CLOUD 2021, http://the cloudcomputing.org/), which was the flagship conference for modeling, developing, publishing, monitoring, managing, and delivering XaaS (everything as a service) in the context of various types of cloud environments.
3. The 2021 International Conference on Big Data (BigData 2021, http://bigdataco ngress.org/), which focused on the scientific and engineering innovations of big data.
4. The 2021 International Conference on Services Computing (SCC 2021, http:// thescc.org/), which was the flagship conference for services innovation lifecycle including enterprise modeling, business consulting, solution creation, services orchestration, services optimization, services management, services marketing, and business process integration and management.

5. The 2021 International Conference on AI and Mobile Services (AIMS 2021, http://ai1000.org/), which addressed the science and technology of artificial intelligence and the development, publication, discovery, orchestration, invocation, testing, delivery, and certification of AI-enabled services and mobile applications.
6. The 2021 World Congress on Services (SERVICES 2021, http://servicescongress.org/), which put its focus on emerging service-oriented technologies and industry-specific services and solutions.
7. The 2021 International Conference on Cognitive Computing (ICCC 2021, http://thecognitivecomputing.org/), which put its focus on Sensing Intelligence (SI) as a Service (SIaaS), making a system listen, speak, see, smell, taste, understand, interact, and/or walk, in the context of scientific research and engineering solutions.
8. The 2021 International Conference on Internet of Things (ICIOT 2021, http://iciot.org/), which addressed the creation of IoT technologies and the development of IOT services.
9. The 2021 International Conference on Edge Computing (EDGE 2021, http://theedgecomputing.org/), which put its focus on the state of the art and practice of edge computing including, but not limited to, localized resource sharing, connections with the cloud, and 5G devices and applications.
10. The 2021 International Conference on Blockchain (ICBC 2021, http://blockchain1000.org/), which concentrated on blockchain-based services and enabling technologies.

Some of the highlights of SCF 2021 were as follows:

– Bigger Platform: The 10 collocated conferences (SCF 2021) got sponsorship from the Services Society which is the world-leading not-for-profits organization (501 c(3)) dedicated to serving more than 30,000 services computing researchers and practitioners worldwide. A bigger platform means bigger opportunities for all volunteers, authors, and participants. In addition, Springer provided sponsorship for best paper awards and other professional activities. All 10 conference proceedings of SCF 2021 will be published by Springer and indexed in the ISI Conference Proceedings Citation Index (included in Web of Science), the Engineering Index EI (Compendex and Inspec databases), DBLP, Google Scholar, IO-Port, MathSciNet, Scopus, and ZBlMath.
– Brighter Future: While celebrating the 2021 version of ICWS, SCF 2021 highlighted the Fourth International Conference on Blockchain (ICBC 2021) to build the fundamental infrastructure for enabling secure and trusted services ecosystems. It will also lead our community members to create their own brighter future.
– Better Model: SCF 2021 continued to leverage the invented Conference Blockchain Model (CBM) to innovate the organizing practices for all 10 collocated conferences.

Contents

Contents

Power Consumption Reduction Method and Edge Offload Server for Multiple Robots

Sannomiya Natsuho[1], Takeshi Ohkawa[2], Hideharu Amano[3], and Midori Sugaya[1](✉)

[1] Shibaura Institute of Technology, 3-7-5 Toyosu, Koto City, Tokyo, Japan
doly@shibaura-it.ac.jp
[2] Tokai University, Takanawa 2-3-23, Minato City, Tokyo, Japan
[3] Keio University, 4-1-1 Hiyoshi, Kohoku-ku, Yokohama-shi, Kanagawa, Japan

Abstract. There are emerging services for the transports and nursing with multiple robots has become more familiar to our society. Considering the increasing demand for automatic multiple robotic services, it appears the research into automatic multiple robotic services is not satisfactory. Specifically, the issues of power consumption of these robots, and its potential reduction have not been sufficiently discussed.

In this research, we propose a method and system to reduce the aggregated power consumption of multiple robots by modelling the characteristics of the hardware and service of each robot. We firstly discuss the prediction model of the robot and improve the formula with consideration of its use in a wide range of situations. Then, we achieve the objective of reducing the aggregate power consumption of multiple robots, using consumption logs and re-allocating tasks of them based on the power consumption prediction model of the individual robot. We propose the design and develop a system using ROS (Robot Operating System) asynchronous server to collect the data from the robots, and make the prediction model for each robot, and reallocate tasks based on the findings of the optimized combination on the server. Through the evaluation of the design and implementation with the proposed system and the actual robot Zoom (GR-PEACH + Rasberry pi), we achieve an average power reduction effect of 14%. In addition, by offloading high-load processing to an edge server configured with FPGA instead the Intel Core i7 performance computer, we achieved and increase in processing speed of up to about 70 times.

Keywords: Total power reduction method · Software system · Power savings · Aggregated power reduction · ROS · Offloading · Multiple robots

1 Introduction

In recent years, multi-robotics services have seen widespread use in various scenarios. In medicine, the surgical intervention robot [1] has seen increased use during the COVID-19 pandemic [2]. Robots for transporting drugs and specimens have been introduced on a trial basis [7]. Security robots are also widely used to fight crime and gained interest from various educational institutions and organizations [3]. Unmanned patrol robots

L.-J, Zhang (Ed.): EDGE 2021, LNCS 12990, pp. 1–19, 2022.
https://doi.org/10.1007/978-3-030-96504-4_1

and surveillance drones are being developed and tested [8]. Robots also work following disasters such as Fukushima, amongst others [4]. In these fields, unmanned vehicles have been developed for searching and moving debris from contaminated areas where it is difficult and dangerous for humans to work [9].

The emerging service for the transport with multiple robots [5] has become more familiar to society [6]. At transport sites, pilots of transport drones have been introduced [10], and luggage transfer robots have been introduced in warehouses [11]. These days, under the sever situation such that of virus threat, robots' services are more important than ever since it is possible for them to work and achieve the same result in place of people. These robots are working without supervision and alleviating the problem of labor shortages at night and on holidays. Especially in Japan, the use of robots is being promoted as part of measures to handle the reduction in the working population due to a declining birthrate and aging population [12]. In these situations, multiple robots' services are increasing, and we expect this trend to continue [13].

Robots are expected to work continuously and automatically without sudden stops caused by a shortage of electrical power. So, the increase in power consumption accompanying the increase in the number of robots used for service implementation, and the need for the sustainable provision of services, means power management is increasingly important. Looking at the increasing operation of security robots and home delivery drones, the number of robots used in the future will be enormous and we need to reduce the power consumption of the entire service to reduce environmental load. However, methods for reducing overall power consumption through power management in a control system for multiple robots have not been sufficiently discussed. In order to study the overall power consumption, the prediction of the power model of each robot must be studied. Some of the research modeling power consumption of computers has already been proposed [14, 15], particularly for modeling CPUs and GPUs, as have methods for improving power consumption. However, modeling the computers linked to motor actuation such as movement implemented to a robot has not been sufficiently discussed. In addition, there are few that target multiple units.

Shimizu [14], Kantake et al. [15] proposed a robot power consumption prediction model and simulated the reduction of the aggregated power consumption of multiple robots by optimizing task allocation based on the prediction model [15]. The contribution of the study presents a simple model for considering the power consumption of actuators on the computer and presents an idea for optimization of changing the combination of tasks for each robot. The proposal was possible to reduce the aggregated power consumption of robots. However, the power consumption prediction model does not apply for all types of robots, so we cannot apply it for other types of robot. Moreover, they only showed the simulation results and not how to evaluate it in the real environment. There is no proposed architecture to achieve the purpose, so we could not evaluate its effectiveness.

In this research, taking into account the issues found with previous research, we firstly examine the power saving prediction model for robot system that have actuators, and (1) propose a universal robot power consumption prediction model and (2) design and develop a system that reduces the aggregated power consumption through the optimization of tasks by exchanging them between multiple robots and (3) evaluate the effectiveness of the idea using the proposed architecture. To achieve the purpose, we designed and developed the ROS (Robot Operating System) service architecture, which automatically collects the log data, creates the prediction model for each robot, then calculates the optimized combination of re-allocation of the tasks for each robot.

Based on the proposal, we designed and implemented the system, and showed the effectiveness of the power reduction method for controlling multiple robots. The results show a 14.81% reduction was achieved. We implemented the part of the algorithm on the offload server, and the calculation performed by a high-speed edge-based computation system using an FPGA [23]. It achieved 70-times better results than that of the general Core i7 personal computer server.

In this paper, we firstly discuss related work in Sect. 2, then issues and proposal are described in Sect. 3. In Sect. 4, we present a server, and client design, then Sect. 5 we show the evaluation of it. Finally, in Sect. 6, we discuss the implementation of the FPGA - the part of the proposed algorithm, then we conclude the paper in Sect. 7.

2 Related Work

Power reduction in computer systems - technologies mainly using hardware - have been proposed. In processor voltage and frequency control, the DVFS (Dynamic Voltage and Frequency Scaling) algorithm that appropriately controls supply voltage and operating frequency is used in many processors [16]. In recent years, motor control with advanced computers has become common. Controlling the width of the pulse wave (duty cycle) in accordance with the magnitude of the input signal and PWM control of the actuator operation during actuator control are also examples of power consumption reduction methods [16]. The methods have not been generalized for the methods of power consumption control of robots over the whole system of application software on CPU and its motor control. Research on power saving for sensors used in robots includes power saving in moving target recognition systems considering power saving [17] and power saving in flight drone position recognition systems [18]. Various power reduction methods have been proposed, such as a dynamic power management method according to the processing load and power reduction by using low-power sensor nodes. However, these are power reduction technologies mainly on the hardware, and do not consider changes in power consumption depending on services after the shipment of the product.

In order to realize more flexible power reduction, software technology is also important [19, 20]. Y. Kim et al. detect and avoid duplicate searches among processors in a multi-threaded core architecture. We proposed a method and were able to minimize power consumption while maintaining the performance by the DVFS method [19]. Hosangadi et al. proposed a technique for reducing power consumption by reducing the number of calculations in array operations through the automatic replacement of computational instructions [20]. Although power reduction by software is not as effective as hardware, there is great merit in cases where it is difficult to change the hardware, or in cases where it is necessary to flexibly respond to post-shipment services, because the control effect can be obtained by software control even after shipment.

There are individual technologies that reduce the power consumption of multiple robots by taking advantage of these methods. Power saving methods such as a system that promotes the power saving operation by monitoring the power consumption and notifying users are presented next. Sakamura and his colleagues proposed a power-saving system development platform called the TK-SLP (Super Low Power Embedded Software Platform) that includes a power consumption monitoring function for embedded devices [21]. As one of the functions of this platform, a mechanism is provided to automatically transmit the electric energy of each embedded system to the system user by the power consumption monitoring function to promote the power saving operation. However, the function is only monitoring, and this mechanism itself does not reduce power consumption.

There is much research on management systems from the viewpoint of efficient operation of multiple robots. Nakagawa and colleagues proposed a management method to continue services by efficiently linking multiple robots with the cloud [22]. This method allocates a lot of work to individuals with a high battery level and secures charging time for individuals with a low battery level. However, there is a problem that the specificity of the prediction model is low.

Abhijet Ravankar et al. proposed a method for efficient charging by setting a robot that performs charging preferentially based on task priority assigned to the robot, battery consumption during work, and remaining battery power [23]. However, these two studies are aimed at service continuation only by optimizing the charging, but reduction of power consumption of multiple robots has not been deeply discussed.

3 Proposal

3.1 Basic Idea of the Prediction Model

Shimizu et al. proposed a method for reducing the overall power consumption of a system using multiple robots [14]. Based on the basic idea, Kantake proposed a prediction model focusing on individual differences between the robots and proposed an optimization method that exchanges the work more accurately [15]. They analyzed the characteristics of the power consumption of robots based on two differences. One is the difference that comes from distinct operations. Even if you have the same type of robots, their power consumption tendency is different if they work in different places or do slightly different operations. For example, robot A works around a wide, low-friction floor, and robot B works on a small, rough floor. They are required to work differently from each other so there will be a different power consumption profile. The second difference is the diverse basic power consumption that comes from the different types of hardware. Even if the robots are the same products, the power consumption tendency is different since the robots may use different electronic parts or the parts have different electric characteristics even it has the same product specification.

Based on the regression prediction model, they propose a method of reducing the aggregated power consumption of the multiple robots. If there is a robot with a model that consumes power at high-speed working on the many tasks, and the other robot that consumes power at low speed with working on the small tasks, the aggregated power would be reduced if they exchanged their tasks [14]. This method was simple and practical for the multiple robot services that are controlled through the server. If the server collects the power consumption logs from each robot and calculates the optimized combination of allocated tasks, the aggregated power consumption for the robots is reduced.

3.2 Issues

Kantake has defined the differences for each robot as "individual differences in hardware" and "individual differences in service (motion)", respectively [15]. Based on this definition, they developed the power consumption prediction model, and implemented the prototype system using multiple iRobot Creates, and executed the task exchange according to the developed prediction model. Their evaluation showed that they succeeded in reducing the aggregated power consumption of the prototype services [15]. However, there is a lack of versatility in the power consumption prediction model, since the model is evaluated only with the iRobot Create. The other problem is that they have not showed the effectiveness of the model through the evaluation of use in an actual environment.

3.3 Proposal

In this research, to solve the problems, we firstly examine the power saving prediction model for robot systems, and (1) propose a generalized model to predict power consumption of a robot with actuators and (2) design and develop a system that achieves a reduction in the aggregated power consumption through the optimization of task exchange between multiple robots and (3) evaluate the effectiveness of the idea using the proposed architecture. To achieve the purpose, we designed and developed the ROS (Robot Operating System) service architecture, and made it automatically collect log data, and create the prediction model for each robot, then, calculate the optimized re-allocation of the tasks for each robot. Additionally, we contribute that (4) reduces the time of the calculation on the server using a high-speed edge-based computation system using an FPGA [23].

3.4 Definition of Power Consumption

We firstly describe the prediction formula from previous research [14]. In the formula, the individual difference was descried as two characteristics of the consumption of the "hardware" and "service" (motion) that can be divided into two parts: basic hardware power consumption and movement distance. In addition, the hardware power consumption when moving and the power consumption during running from stop to the two states are expressed as the power consumption [15]. The power consumption W of a certain individual X is calculated by the following Eq. (1).

$$W = d \times CPDx + r \times CPSx \qquad (1)$$

In the Formula 1, d is moving distance, r is number of transitions from the stop state to the running state, CPDx (individual x, and the power consumption of rate with a moving distance), CPSx (individual x, and power consumption of per the number of times the moving state from a stopped state) [14]. The prediction of consumed power of a robot is estimated from the formula. The *d* and *r* are observed and should be set. The CPDx and CPSx had been calculated before the prediction [15].

3.4.1 Estimation of Travel Distance by Changing Battery Voltage

In the Kantake model shown in Formula 1, the moving distance of the robot changes according to the physical environment conditions. In addition, since there are many robots that cannot directly measure the distance traveled, it was considered that a model with higher versatility would be one that evaluated energy consumed during the movement. Therefore, we proposed a new calculation that focuses on the energy consumed during the motion. We defined the power consumption (W), expressed by the reduction in battery voltage. Battery voltage: V (v), ratio to the voltage applied to the motor driver: B, wheel diameter: R (cm), average duty ratio applied to the left and right motors: D, maximum rotation speed of the motor and the voltage at that time is multiplied by the proportionality constant of X and the operation time: T (s) to obtain the moving distance of the individual x: Lx (cm) (2).

$$L_x \sum_{i=0}^{T} V \times B \times X \times R \times \pi \times D \tag{2}$$

3.4.2 Verification of Prediction Formula by Actual Machine

To verify the newly proposed prediction equation (2), we verified the actual machine using eight Zumos. The Zumo [7] uses AA batteries, so it is easy to secure rechargeable batteries and charging. The driving time for the battery is long because the small robot uses a low current, and the programming very flexible with Arduino or mbed. For experiments, Zumo has been extended so that voltage can be acquired (Fig. 1).

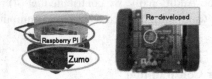

Fig. 1. Zumo Raspberry Pi configuration

We used 8 Zumo units running until 100 cm distance was measured, based on Formula 2. The error between the measured distance and the predicted distance that was calculated on the Formula 2 is as shown in the figure below (Fig. 2).

In the result, the error is considered to be due to the load on the motor shaft due to gravity and the friction of the road surface. Although there is variation among individuals, in Formula 2 the error was 20% to 30%. We make corrections to the distance formula through multiple regression analysis. The theoretical distance value (L_x), measuring the variation of the voltage (VL_x), and maximum voltage during measurement (VmL_x) from the moving distance of less value was calculated to correct the error. The Formula 3 is showing the calibrated distance.

Calibration Distance $= -38.084 + 0.643 \times Lx - 20.487 \times VLx + 10.003 \times VmLx$

$$\tag{3}$$

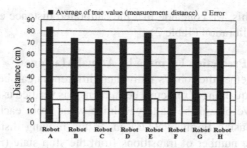

Fig. 2. Error comparison between theoretical and true values

As a result of the calibration by using Formula 3, the average error rate was 4.28%, a reduction of about 87%. In the multiple regression equation evaluation, the multiple determination coefficient was 0.941, the significant F value was low, and the results of the calibrating equation were high (Table 1).

Table 1. Analysis results of multiple regression equation

Multiple regression coefficients*	Multiple determination coefficient*	F value*
0.970	0.941	F < 0.000001

Table 2 shows the effect of each element on the multiple regression equation. The theoretical value (Lx) indicating the estimated distance and the maximum voltage (VmLx during measurement) among the three elements of theoretical value (Lx), amount of change in voltage during measurement (VLx), and maximum voltage during measurement (VmLx).

Table 2. Influence of each element on the multiple regression equation

Lx : Theoretical value (estimated distance)		
Standard Error	**T Value**	**p Value**
0.02	29.14	p<0.0001
VLx : Voltage change during measurement		
Standard Error	**T Value**	**p Value**
8.13	-2.52	0.013
Vm_{Lx} : Maximum voltage during measurement		
Standard Error	**T Value**	**p Value**
4.19	2.39	0.018

As seen in the Table 2, the two values (voltage change and maximum voltage) have a large influence on the moving distance. On the other hand, the amount of voltage change during measurement has a small effect. This is thought that one measurement time is short, and the voltage change is small. However, for all three elements, the p-value is less than 5%. From this, we conclude that the calibrated distance equation in Eq. 3 is appropriate for the calibration (Table 2).

3.4.3 Verification of Prediction Formula by Actual Machine

In order to verify whether the robot's individual differences can be detected from the power consumption equation (Wx), actual equipment was verified using a small endless-track robot Zumo. We obtain the battery voltage value from each Zumo robot, and calculate the values using Formula 2. Based on the moving distance (d) measured in Sect. 3.4.1 and the number of transitions from the stop state (r) and calculate the result as power consumption (W), we calculated the cumulative voltage change with the Formula 1.

3.4.4 Result

The result is shown in Fig. 3 The parameters that simulating the aggregated amount of voltage change every 0.1 s with d = 1000 cm and r = 50. It uses the prediction formula that reflects the revisions. The results are arranged in ascending order of aggregated power consumption.

The variance of variation in power consumption of Zumo was 6.78 (W). Since there is sufficient variation, the versatility of the prediction formula was confirmed. The columns are arranged in ascending order of power consumption, but there was no difference in the order even when the number of stops was fixed, and the moving distance was increased. On the other hand, if the moving distance is fixed and the number of the stops are increased, the order may change. This means the electromotive force required to start rotating the motor in Zumo greatly differs between individual units, affecting the power consumption.

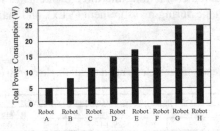

Fig. 3. Cumulative voltage change (W)

3.5 Modeling Power Consumption of Communication

In the proposed prediction formulas in the existing research [15], power consumption of each robot was predicted by two factors: "moving distance" and "number of transitions from moving state to stopped state". However, in services using multiple robots, it is necessary to communicate with the management system and provide feedback on the operation based on data obtained from state determination of each individual and sensors. In recent years, wireless communication utilized for the purpose of avoiding the physical limitation of the robot operation in such communication. It is assumed that the robot in this study is a system that communicates with the central system by receiving commands by the task allocation optimization processing, feedback of sensor values, and transmission of acquired data. In this communication, necessary devices (wireless communication units) and the systems that control them also consume power. Therefore, we modeled the effect of wireless communication on power consumption and improved the accuracy of the prediction formula by adding those elements to the prediction formula proposed in the previous research.

3.6 Experiment Overview

We verify the presence or absence of wireless communication and the effect of the amount of communication per hour on power consumption. The experiments were performed using Zumo and the GR-PEACH, a single computer with a wireless LAN function. Table 3 below shows the specifications of GR-PEACH.

Table 3. GR-PEACH specification

Microcomputer	ARM Cortex-A RZ/A1H
RAM	10 MB
Supported platforms	mbed, Arduino, TOPPERS/ASP, .NET MF
Wireless LAN controller	Rohm BP3595 (2.4 Ghz)
Communication standards	IEEE 802.11 b/g/n
Other	SD card slot pin for Arduino Uno

The following four patterns of operations were executed, and the effect on power consumption examined.

1. Not connected to the network.
2. Authenticate and connect to the wireless LAN access point.
3. After connecting, execute the 100 KB communication in one minute.
4. After making the connection, execute the 1 MB communication in one minute.

Figure 4 shows the result of the four patterns of experiments with eight Zumo units.
The voltage drops when the network was not connected was small, and the power consumption tended to increase as the amount of communication to the network increased. However, the Zumo robots with the largest power consumption (machines 6 and 9) connected to the AP, and the Zumo with a 100 KB communication volume consumes more power than a 1 MB communication volume (frame 2). Variation was observed. The standard deviation was 3.1% when not connected, 3.8% for connection to the AP, 2.8% for 100 KB communication, and 6.1% for 1 MB communication. There is also variation in the increase in power consumption due to the increase in traffic, which can be considered as the individual difference in power consumption of the entire GR-PEACH including the wireless communication unit.

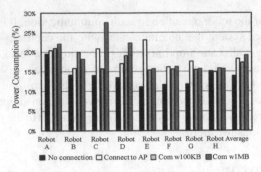

Fig. 4. Measurement result

3.7 Predictive Model Generation

Experiments show that the traffic can be incorporated into the power consumption prediction model. Using the method of the power consumption prediction formula, a prediction formula was calculated for robot 1 used in the previous experiment, considering the communication volume and communication time.

A travel distance of 100 to 500 cm and a communication amount of 100 to 500 KB are specified at random and run until the specified travel distance is reached. The robot is stopped for 0.5 s with a probability of 1/100 every 0.1 s during the run, and the number of stops is counted. After running the specified travel distance, the specified data is sent to the server. Using this as a set, each time one set is completed, the moving distance, the number of stops (number of transitions), the amount of communication, and the time taken for communication are recorded. Multiple regression analysis was performed based on the recorded data, and a new power consumption prediction formula was calculated. Formula 4 is the result of adding the product of the power consumption per 1 KB of communication volume $CPCx$ [%] and the aggregated traffic volume during operation (n) [KB] added to the existing power consumption prediction formula.

$$Wx = d \times CPDx + r \times CPSx + n \times CPCx \tag{4}$$

As for the multiple correlation, prediction formula 4 considering communication was improved by 0.3% compared to when it was not used. Table 4 shows the analysis results for each element.

The absolute values of the t-values are all $p < 0.5*$ or more, and the three explanatory variables are considered to be sufficiently effective. From the result, we conclude that the power consumption prediction formula considering the traffic volume has increased accuracy and significance compared to the existing prediction formula.

4   Optimization Processing by Edge Offload Server

4.1   Reduction Method by Task Allocation

Based on the improved power consumption prediction model, we try to reduce the aggregated power consumption of the multiple robots through the actual implementation service by the running the operation with the allocation optimization method.

Table 4. Multiple regression analysis results for each element

Moving distance		
Standard error	T value	p value
1.24E−06	−14.67	1.67E−42
Number of transitions		
Standard error	T value	p value
4.81E−05	9.28	2.34E−19
Traffic		
Standard error	T value	p value
5.74E−07	16.15	7.61E−50

For the optimal task allocation that is explained in Sect. 3.1 that appeared firstly in [14, 15], we developed a prototype system. In the system, the data is collected from the individual robots, and the optimal motion allocation is determined based on the prediction formula. Specifically, it is a method to allocate fewer tasks to individuals with the higher power consumption rate and allocate more tasks to individuals with the lower power consumption rate calculated by the prediction formula. The basic algorithm is presented in the existing research, and we apply the algorithm to the server client system. In this research, we verify the optimal task allocation based on the predicted value at the time of operation by the actual machine which was not implemented in the previous research [15].

4.2 System Design and Implementation

The data collection and allocation action process are mainly executed by the server (Fig. 5). These aggregation results are processed on the server and the task sorting applied. Therefore, we decided to develop a server-client type asynchronous distributed processing system. Processing on the server consists of two stages: firstly, the robot is registered on the server, then, it starts to work: (1) it receives the task command sent from the server. According to the instruction, the robot executes the task. If it finished the instructed work, it (2) sends the data to the server. Then, (3) the server accepts the data from the client, (4) calculates the predicted model based on the prediction formulas and on the data that collected from individual robots, and (5), (6) executes allocation optimization based on the prediction formulas. Table 5 summarizes the details of the processing.

The robot is equipped with a motor, a control microcomputer (Arduino), and communication and control (Raspberry Pi). In addition, it can issue instructions and transmit data using general-purpose communication middleware ROS (Robot Operating System) [24], which provides the asynchronous communications and general publish/subscribe communication mechanism (i.e. pub/sub) to achieve the generalized interface for these kinds of services. Figure 5 shows a diagram of the implemented system. Both the server

Table 5. Details of server/client (robot) processing

Robot
(1) Receive the task command sent from the server and execute the task according to the instruction.
(2) At the end of each task, robot (client) sends to the server three data items: the distance traveled, the number of transitions from the stopped state to the driving, and the battery voltage.

Server
(3) Read data sent from the robot (client),
(4) Perform the prediction formula calculation of power consumption based on the moved distance of each robot, the number of transitions from the stopped state to the operating state, and the battery voltage. Multiple regression analysis is performed too.
(5) Calculate the optimal task combination based on the power consumption value for each robot from the obtained prediction formula. The optimal task is to perform quick sort in ascending order of power consumption.
(6) Determination of task allocation and transmit results.

(edge computer) and the client (robot) used ROS on Linux and realized with ROS on Linux data transmission and reception by pub/sub communication [24].

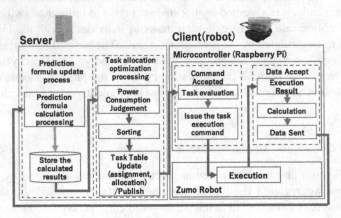

Fig. 5. Server client design

5   Evaluation

5.1   Overview of the Evaluation

Based on the prediction model of the power consumption formula, we developed a server client system using the ROS (pub/sub) middleware. Then, we evaluated the aggregated power consumption reduction effect in the developed system through the task allocation optimization process executed on the server. We verify the optimization effect by comparing the aggregated power consumptions on the different types of the batteries when task allocation optimization processing using 10 Zumo machines. The system configuration is shown the Table 6, and the experimental evaluation picture in the Fig. 6.

Table 6. Evaluation environment

	CPU	Memory	OS
Server	Intel® Core™ i7-4600U (1.8 GHz)	8.0 GB	Ubuntu 16.04 LTS
Client	ARMCortexA53 (1.4 Ghz)	1.0 GB	UbuntuMate 18.04 LTS

The tasks assigned to the robot in this experiment consist of four actions: forward, backward, left turn, and right turn.

Fig. 6. Experimental of actual robotics evaluation system

We developed the 10 sets of Zumo robots that operate according to the detail in Table 7. Each Zumo changed the time taken for the operation and the total number of sets. Changes in total travel time and distance, and total number of transitions are shown at the Table 7.

Table 7. Execution task list

Task	1st Set	2nd set	3rd Set	4th Set	5th Set	6th Set	Total number of transitions
1	1 sec	—	—	—	—	4 sec	4 times
2	2 sec	—	—	—	—	8 sec	4 times
3	1 sec	2 sec	—	—	—	12 sec	8 times
4	2 sec	2 sec	—	—	—	16 sec	8 times
5	1 sec	2 sec	2 sec	—	—	20 sec	12 times
6	2 sec	2 sec	2 sec	—	—	24 sec	12 times
7	1 sec	2 sec	2 sec	2 sec	—	28 sec	16 times
8	2 sec	2 sec	2 sec	2 sec	—	32 sec	16 times
9	1 sec	2 sec	2 sec	2 sec	2 sec	36 sec	20 times
10	2 sec	2 sec	2 sec	2 sec	2 sec	40 sec	20 times

In the optimization process of task allocation in this experiment, the robots were sorted in descending order of power consumption. Based on the sorting results, the task with the least amount of work was assigned to the robot with the highest power consumption, and the task with the highest amount of the work was assigned to the robot with the lowest power consumption. In this way, the allocation optimization processing was executed according to their volume of power consumption.

5.2 Experimental Results (with Nickel Hydrogen Battery)

Figure 7 shows the experimental results with a nickel hydrogen battery. It shows the cumulative power consumption and the ratio of the reduction effect for 4 h from the measurement start time (when the robot operation started).

The rate of reduction reached a peak about 3 h (180 min) from the start. On the other hand, after the peak, the reduction effect decreased, that is, no reduction effect was observed. The average reduction effect over the entire four hours was 14.81%, which was a sufficiently large reduction effect compared to the reduction effect of 0.22% that was confirmed in experiments in the previous research using the different robot, such as the iRobot [14, 23]. It means that the individual difference of the hardware of Zumo is more remarkable than iRobot Create used in the Kantake's results [14]. Another reason is that Zumo was able to generate highly accurate prediction formulas due to the longer duration of data collection. In the experiment with Zumo, we collected the working data for 4 h, whereas, in contrast, the iRobot Create experiment by Kantake's collected data only for one hour so it would make the low prediction model from the working data.

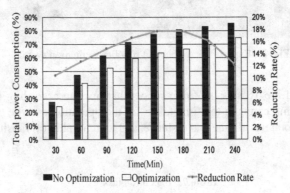

Fig. 7. Comparison of power consumption with and without task allocation optimization for 10 units of robots using nickel metal hydride battery

5.3 Experimental Results (with Alkaline Battery)

We tried to investigate the effect of the reduction in different type of battery, for example, an alkaline battery. Figure 8 shows the results when the same experiment as in Fig. 7 was performed using an alkaline battery.

The power consumption when using alkaline batteries was more than twice that of nickel-metal hydride batteries. The reduction effect was about 7% at the start but decreased over time. The average reduction effect over the entire 4 h was about − 0.06%, indicating that there was almost no reduction effect. It is thought that the higher power consumption per hour of alkaline batteries compared to nickel-metal hydride was related to the lack of reduction effect.

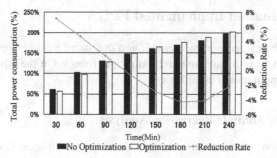

Fig. 8. Comparison of power consumption with and without task allocation optimization 10 units of robots using alkaline batteries

5.4 Discussion

There was a difference in the aggregated power consumption reduction effect depending on the battery used and the usage time. The reason for this result can be explained by the effect of the discharge characteristics of the battery. Figure 9 shows the discharge characteristics of the nickel-metal hydride battery. As shown in the figure, the discharge shows a linear drop curve up to a certain voltage as time passes. However, at some point the voltage drop will be steep. The voltage value when the voltage starts to drop sharply and the elapsed time from the time of full charge are affected not only by the individual difference of the battery itself but also by the total number of charges and discharges. Therefore, the timing at which the voltage begins to drop does not always coincide.

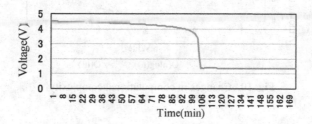

Fig. 9. Discharge characteristics of nickel-metal hydride battery

Similarly, alkaline batteries draw a non-linear falling curve during discharge, which suggests that the aggregated power consumption was not reduced. From this fact, to maximize the effect of the task allocation optimization process, we must address the following:

1. Monitor that the voltage drop curve of the battery has a nearly linear characteristic
2. If the voltage drop curve deviates significantly from the linear, it is necessary to temporarily remove it from the task allocation optimization process for charging.

If the conditions are satisfied, it is possible to obtain the better reduction effect on the system.

6 System Evaluation Implemented FPGA

In this research, we designed, implemented, and evaluated a highly versatile task allocation optimization system that can handle multiple robots. On the other hand, there is the problem its computational complexity.

6.1 Complexity of Multiple Regression Analysis

In the task allocation optimization system, we use the multiple regression analysis as a method of calculating the power consumption prediction formula from the robot log data. In the experiments in this study, the number of voltage changes was set as the Y value. And the moving distance and the number of transitions were set as the X value. Multiple regression analysis has been performed based on the X and Y elements.

The number of X values greatly affects the total number of calculations for multiple regression analysis and sorting. Let n be the total number of robots to be calculated. When the X value is one, the order of computation is $O(n \log n)$. However, when there are two X values, the order of computation becomes $O(n!)$. Figure 10 is a graph showing the change in the number of calculations on the vertical axis due to the change in the value of n.

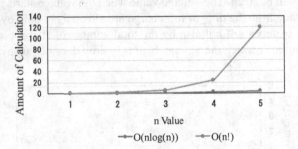

Fig. 10. Changes in computational complexity

When there are two X values, the number of calculations will explode as the total number of robots increases. In this experiment, the amount of 3,628,800 for the 10 robots was calculated using the server with the specifications shown in Table 8 below. However, no problems such as processing taking more than 1 s were observed.

Table 8. Calculation server specifications

CPU	Intel® Core™ i7-4600U (1.8 GHz)
RAM	8.0 GB
OS	Ubunutu 16.04 LTS
SSD	M.2. SATA3 SSD

However, as the number of robots increases, the number of calculations becomes enormous. But it is difficult to reduce the amount of computation overload. A dedicated calculation system for processing a huge amount of calculation is required. Therefore, we examine the difference in processing time from a normal computer with a high-speed computing system using an FPGA on the FiC board [22], which employs Xilinx's FPGA device XCKU095 (Mark2 xcku115-flvb2104-2-e: m2fic00-m2fic11). On the FiC board, RaspberryPi3 works as the programming controller of the FPGA device and the host for data communication with FPGA through GPIO port. The Multiple Regression Analysis (MRAS) processing is implemented in C++ and synthesized into HDL by using Vivado HLS 2019.1.

6.2 Experimental Procedure

We developed a FPGA processing circuit for the multiple regression analysis program based on the calculation of the formula 1 and 2, and compare the execution times (Fig. 11).

```
// constant is 0, two X values are used (x1, x2)
from i = 0 to the total number of robots Read data of robot i
    // Data is defined for each line as "y, x1, x2"
    // the coefficient of x1 is k1 and the coefficient of x2 is k2
    maximum number of rows from for j = 0
        a += y × x1
        b += y × x2
        c += x1 × x2
        d += x1 × x1
        e += x2 × x2
        a-d * k1-c * k2 = 0
        b-c * k1-e * k2 = 0
    //Find the coefficients k1 and k2 from the above two simultaneous equations
```

Fig. 11. Multiple regression analysis algorithm

The specifications of the computer to be compared are the same as those in Table 3. Table 5 compares the average processing time taken for a single multiple regression analysis for a single multiple regression analysis of a CSV file with 539 lines. Experiments were conducted to eliminate the effects of GPIO communication, extra processing and cache that are not required for calculations such as screen display (Table 9).

Table 9. Comparison of multiple regression analysis execution times

	FPGA	PC
Average time (μ sec)	32.28 (μ sec)	2410.3 (μ sec)

The processing speed of the FPGA was 70-times faster than that of the PC. From these results, it is thought that on-time calculation processing can be realized even under conditions closer to the real environment by speeding up the calculation processing by FPGA.

7 Conclusion

In this paper, we consider the problems of previous research, and proposed a method that has the effect of reducing the aggregated power consumption by using Zumo. Based on the proposal, we designed and implemented the system, and showed the effectiveness of the power reduction method for controlling multiple robots. The results show a 14.81% reduction was achieved. We implemented the part of the algorithm on the offload server, and the calculation performed by a high-speed edge-based computation system using an FPGA [23]. The FPGA implementation of task optimization processing showed that The processing speed of the FPGA was 32.28 us, which was 70 times higher than that of the PC.

In the future, we will carry out verification for the experiments on actual equipment based on these prediction formulas with changing conditions and verify the timing of optimization processing that can maximize the reduction effect.

Acknowledgments. This research was supported by Japan Science and Technology Agency (JST), CREST, JPMJCR19K1.

References

1. Burgner-Kahrs, J., et al.: Continuum robots for medical applications: a survey. IEEE Trans. Rob. **31**(6), 1261–1280 (2015)
2. Zemmar, A., Lozano, A.M., Nelson, B.J.: The rise of robots in surgical environments during COVID-19. Nature Machine Intelligence, vol. 2, pp. 566–572 (2020)
3. Teodoros, T., Hu, H.: Toward intelligent security robots: a survey. IEEE Trans. Syst. Man Cybern. Part C (Appl. Rev.) **42**(6), 1261–1280 (2012)
4. Sakaue, T., et al.: Survey in Fukushima Daiichi NPS by combination of human and remotely-controlled robot. In: IEEE International Symposium on Safety, Security and Rescue Robotics, pp. 11–13 (2017)
5. Kiva Systems: Three Engineers, Hundreds of Robots, One Warehouse. IEEE Spectrum. https://spectrum.ieee.org/robotics/robotics-software/three-engineers-hundreds-of-robots-one-warehouse. Accessed 07 Jan 2020
6. Maneewarn, T., et al.: Survey of Social Robots in Thailand. International Electrical Engineering Congress (iEECON), pp. 19–21 (2014)
7. Hospie | Panasonic Collaboration II Co-production | Matsushita Memorial Hospital. http://phio.panasonic.co.jp/kinen/pc/hospi/index.htm. Accessed 07 Jan 2020
8. Japan's first patrol monitoring service for SECOM drone, an autonomous flight surveillance robot SECOM drone that completely autonomously starts, flies, returns, and recharges. PFI prison "Mine Societies" in which SECOM participates as a representative company Start on March 1 at the "Return Promotion Center" SECOM Corporation. https://www.secom.co.jp/corporate/release/2017/nr_20180301.html. Accessed 07 Jan 2020

9. Disaster response robot Quince | TadoLab. Tohoku University Human-Robot Informatics Laboratory. https://www.rm.is.tohoku.ac.jp/quince_mech/#Quince_1. Accessed 07 Jan 2020
10. Starting inter-post office transport using small unmanned aerial vehicles. Japan Post. https://www.post.japanpost.jp/notification/pressrelease/2018/00_honsha/1030_01.html. Accessed 07 Jan 2020
11. Amazon Uses 800 Robots to Run This Warehouse. IEEE Spectrum. https://spectrum.ieee.org/automaton/robotics/industrial-robots/amazon-introduces-two-new-warehouse-robots. Accessed 07 Jan 2020
12. Ministry of Economy, Trade and Industry. New Strategy for Robots, 2015 edn. (2015) http://warp.da.ndl.go.jp/info:ndljp/pid/11181294/www.meti.go.jp/committee/sankoushin/seizou/pdf/003_s01_03.pdf. Accessed 25 Dec 2019
13. New Energy and Industrial Technology Development Organization. Future market forecast for the robot industry toward 2035 (2010). https://www.nedo.go.jp/content/100080673.pdf. Accessed 25 Dec 2019
14. Shimizu, K., et al.: Proposal of management method based on motion and power consumption characteristics of multiple distributed mobile robots. In: IPSJ 78th National Convention (2015)
15. Kantake, T.: Distributed task processing considering rmption of multiple robots. In: Embedded Systems Symposium 2018 Proceedings, pp. 108–109 (2018)
16. Takasu, M., et al.: Evaluation of power saving mechanism in embedded processors. In: Embedded System Symposium 2012, pp. 79–86 (2012)
17. Pan, S., et al.: A low-power soc-based moving target detection system for amphibious spherical robot. In: IEEE International Conference on Mechatronics and Automation (ICMA), pp. 1116–1121 (2015)
18. Eckert, J., et al.: An indoor localization framework for four-rotor flying robots using low-power sensor nodes. IEEE Trans. Instrum. Meas. 60(2), 336–344 (2011)
19. Kim, Y., et al.: BRAIN: a low-power deep search engine for autonomous robots. IEEE Micro 37(5), 11–19 (2017)
20. Hosangadi, A., et al.: Energy efficient hardware synthesis of polynomial expressions. In: 18th International Conference on VLSI Design, pp. 653–658 (2005)
21. Sakamura, K.: Research and development of TK-SLP (T-KernelSuper-LowPower) embedded software platform (2014). http://www.soumu.go.jp/main_content/000323271.pdf. Accessed 07 Jan 2020
22. Create 2 Programmable RobotliRobot. https://www.irobot.com/about-irobot/stem/create-2. Accessed 07 Jan 2020
23. Musha, K., Kudoh, T., Amano, H.: Deep learning on high performance FPGA switching boards: flow-in-cloud. In: Proceedings of International Symposium on Applied Reconfigurable Computing (2018)
24. Quigley, M., Gerkey, B., Smart, W.D.: Programming Robots with ROS, O'Reilly Media (2015). ISBN 9781449323899

Sparta: Heat-Budget-Based Scheduling Framework on IoT Edge Systems

Michael Zhang[✉], Chandra Krintz, and Rich Wolski

Department of Computer Science, University of California,
Santa Barbara, CA 93106, USA
{lebo,ckrintz,rich}@cs.ucsb.edu

Abstract. Co-location of processing infrastructure and IoT devices at the edge is used to reduce response latency and long-haul network use for IoT applications. As a result, edge clouds for many applications (e.g. agriculture, ecology, and smart city deployments) must operate in remote, unattended, and environmentally harsh settings, introducing new challenges. One key challenge is heat exposure, which can degrade the performance, reliability, and longevity of electronics. For edge clouds, these problems are exacerbated because they increasingly perform complex workloads, such as machine learning, to affect data-driven actuation and control of devices and systems in the environment.

The goal of our work is to protect edge clouds from overheating. To enable this, we develop a heat-budget-based scheduling system, called Sparta, which leverages dynamic voltage and frequency scaling (DVFS) to adaptively control CPU temperature. Sparta takes machine learning applications, datasets, and a temperature threshold as input. It sets the initial frequency of the CPU based on historical data and then dynamically updates it, according to the applications' execution profile and ambient temperature, to safeguard edge devices. We find that for a suite of machine learning applications and deployment temperatures, Sparta is able to maintain CPU temperature below the threshold 94% of the time while facilitating improvements in execution time by $1.04x - 1.32x$ over competitive approaches.

Keywords: Edge computing · Heat budget · Scheduling system · IoT

1 Introduction

The Internet of Things (IoT) is a rapidly emerging set of technologies in which ordinary objects are equipped with digital intelligence – the ability to sense, analyze, and control their environment automatically. By linking the physical and digital worlds, IoT has the potential to enhance situational awareness and effective decision-making by humans, to detect, diagnose, and remediate problems without human intervention, to assist with personal and homeland security, to optimize manufacturing and business processes, and to automate operations throughout the economy.

© Springer Nature Switzerland AG 2022
L.-J. Zhang (Ed.): EDGE 2021, LNCS 12990, pp. 20–34, 2022.
https://doi.org/10.1007/978-3-030-96504-4_2

To realize this impact, IoT must be embedded in the world around us – within buildings, cars, roads, homes, industrial machinery, and waterways, and distributed across farms, wild open spaces, cities, and oceans. Moreover, they increasingly leverage recent advances in data analytics, machine learning (ML), and automation *in-situ* – at the edge of the network – "near" (in terms of network latency) the locus of sensing and/or actuation. This move to the edge is the result of an increase in the velocity and volume of data and high response latencies imposed by the long-haul, intermittently available networks that connect the edge and cloud. Further, unlike in the context of e-commerce and other cloud application domains, IoT applications often benefit from spatial locality in terms of performance, robustness, and security. That is, co-location of processing infrastructure and IoT devices significantly reduces the latency between data acquisition and device actuation, enables the extension of device capability via local offloading, and alleviates the cost, power consumption, and congestion of network use versus the centralized, cloud-direct model [1].

Edge processing, however, introduces new challenges for IoT deployments. Unlike the devices themselves, edge computing elements are often designed for environments in which the ambient environmental conditions are controlled and kept within a narrow operational range. The operational settings in which these edge systems (in our work we deploy miniaturized "edge clouds" using clusters of commodity small-board computers to support IoT analytics) are deployed can be harsh, hard or costly to access, and exposed to harmful environmental elements (heat, moisture, dust, animals, other objects, humans, weather, etc.). For example, we currently support an IoT deployment for image processing and deep learning for the automatic, real-time identification of animals using camera traps deployed across UCSB Sedgwick Reserve, an ecology and wildlife educational and research reserve in California [2]. The reserve is 6,000 acres that comprise critical wildlife habitats, two watersheds at the foot of Figueroa Mountain in Santa Ynez, California, and a 300-acre farm easement. Our edge clouds fuse and analyze images from within out-buildings on the property. Sedgwick yearly outdoor temperatures range between 30° and 116° F (−1.1° to 46.7° C); within enclosures (e.g. shelters for electrical pumping equipment where grid electricity is available) our cloud systems are subjected to much higher ambient operating temperatures.

Excessive heat can degrade the performance and reliability of devices and negatively impact their longevity (requiring more human intervention and frequent replacement). Commodity computers are particularly sensitive to high temperatures and extended exposure can cause these machines to break down, degrade in functionality, and fail prematurely – even they are protected using operational safeguards such as throttling and automatic shutdown [3]. For this reason, most manufacturers include an on-board thermal CPU temperature sensor and the ability to set a "shut-down" temperature if the CPU exceeds the manufacturer's maximum supported temperature. Figure 1 shows a time series of CPU temperature in degrees Fahrenheit gathered from one of our edge clouds deployed at Sedgwick between February 2018 and June 2020. The cut-off tem-

perature was set to 200 °F (93.3 °C) and the temperature drop early in the trace
records the system's automatic shutdown.

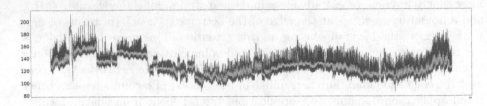

Fig. 1. The time series of CPU temperature in the edge cloud deployed at Sedgwick
Natural Reserve from Feb. 28th, 2018 to Jun. 3rd, 2020. The x-axis is the epoch time
and the y-axis is the CPU temperature in Fahrenheit.

In this paper, we investigate the use of dynamic voltage and frequency scaling (DVFS) [4,5] to control system temperature when the ambient temperature
might cause it to exceed the acceptable operational range. DVFS is a technique
that has been widely studied in the context of "power capping" – the implementation of a maximum power draw by the system. Our system – called *Sparta*
– automatically exploits the relationship between system power consumption
and generated heat. It does so by adjusting processor frequency dynamically so
that CPU temperatures do not exceed a specified threshold as ambient temperature changes. Subject to the threshold, the system attempts to minimize the
application "slow down" (relative to maximum CPU frequency) that frequency
adjustments might introduce. We use Sparta to study the relationships between
CPU frequency, temperature, power dissipation, and execution behavior. Moreover, we consider IoT workloads that employ a wide range of machine learning
algorithms, including image recognition, natural language processing, decision
forest, and time series prediction.

We consider three modes for the Sparta frequency scheduler: **Annealing**,
AIMD, and **Hybrid**. Annealing employs an epsilon-greedy strategy to extrapolate an appropriate CPU frequency in real time. AIMD uses the linear growth of
CPU frequency when temperature is under threshold and exponential reduction
when it detects temperature anomalies to determine its CPU frequency. With
Hybrid, we combine the best features of the two modes to overcome their draw-
backs. Our results show that Sparta in Hybrid mode speeds up the execution
of our applications by **1.16x** and **1.14x** on average in three thermal environments compared to Annealing and AIMD. Moreover, Sparta in Hybrid mode
maintains CPU temperature below threshold **94.4%** of the time (as measured
via temperature sampling), on average across all benchmarks.

In summary, with this paper, we make the following contributions:

– We investigate the relationship between CPU frequency and sampling temperature to precisely model and manage processor power dissipation during
  execution;

- We design and implement a heat-budget-based scheduling framework that protects edge systems from overheating and potential damage;
- We empirically evaluate the efficacy of using Sparta to control CPU temperature and accelerate machine learning applications on six real-world benchmarks in three thermal deployment environments.

In the following sections, we present the design and implementation of Sparta (Sect. 2). We then describe our experimental methodology and empirical evaluation of the system using multiple machine learning applications in different thermal environments (Sect. 3). In Sect. 4, we discuss related work. Finally, we present our conclusions and future work plans.

2   Sparta

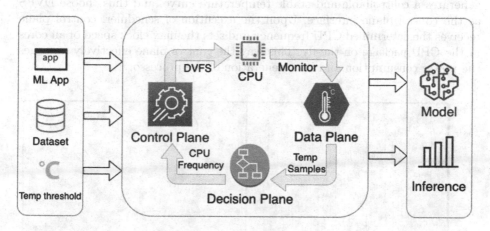

Fig. 2. The architecture of Sparta

2.1   Architecture

To address the processor overheating challenge and accelerate the execution of applications under a CPU temperature threshold, we develop Sparta, a heat-budget-based scheduling framework for edge devices and machine learning applications. The architecture of Sparta is shown in Fig. 2. The scheduler consists of three components: a control plane, a data plane, and a decision plane. Sparta takes a machine learning application, datasets, and a CPU temperature threshold as input. During the execution, the scheduler utilizes a feedback control mechanism that controls the CPU temperature by dynamically adjusting CPU frequency via system-level dynamic voltage and frequency scaling (DVFS). Sparta returns the trained model and inference results at the end of the execution.

The data plane monitors, samples, and records the CPU real-time temperature via the lm-sensors interface [6] and selects the maximum temperature within a sliding time window. Both the sampling rate and window size are configurable. (1/second and 5 s by default) To signify the authentic temperature of multi-core processors, data plane records the temperature samples of the entire CPU package instead of any specific ones. Being accessible by decision plane, all structured temperature data helps determine the proper CPU frequency in real time to keep the CPU temperature under threshold.

The control plane manages the CPU power and temperature. In the design phase, we consider two methods: Sleep injection and DVFS. The first method injects sleep time in the iteration loop that lowers the CPU usage, whereas the second method adjusts the CPU frequency by tuning the CPU voltage. We experiment with these two methods on a multi-threaded matrix multiplication benchmark and monitor the CPU temperature. Figure 3 shows the CPU temperature time series using these two methods. We observe the latter method generates a controllable and stable temperature curve, and thus choose DVFS as the control plane interface. Upon the execution of scheduler, control plane receives the determined CPU frequency and sets the max clock speed of all cores in the CPU package on-the-fly. This way the control plane effectively manages the power consumption and heat generation of the processor.

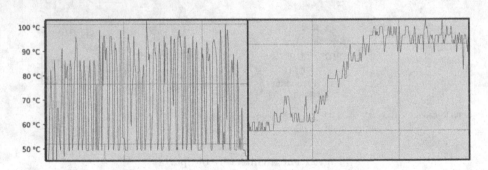

Fig. 3. The CPU temperature time series by sleep injection (left) vs DVFS (right). The x-axis is the time frame and the y-axis is the CPU temperature ranging from 48 °C to 100 °C.

The decision plane determines the CPU frequency based on historical and real-time temperature data throughout the execution. To provide the historical dataset, on which decision plane decides the initial CPU frequency, we collect CPU temperature and frequency data from a multi-threaded matrix multiplication (MATMUL) benchmark that simulates the underlying operations in machine learning applications.

We gather the data in the ambient temperature ranging from 2.6 °C to 43.8 °C to cover different thermal environments. In the experiment, we found the sequence of CPU frequency and maximum temperature in a time window demonstrate a better linear relationship than the sequence of all temperature, because of its inherent oscillating feature. To verify the correlation between MATMUL and machine learning applications, we collect the same data from an image recognition application written in Tensorflow [7]. As depicted in Fig. 4, we found the correlated linear relationship between the CPU frequency and logarithmic delta temperature defined as $log(T_{max} - T_i)$, where T_{max} is the maximum temperature sample in the time window and T_i is the starting CPU temperature in idle state.

Depending on this correlation, decision plane extrapolates the appropriate CPU frequency by linear regression from the MATMUL dataset and assigns initial CPU frequency before the execution starts. During the process, decision plane starts to extrapolate CPU frequency from real-time data that accurately reflects the ambient temperature and the execution pattern of ML applications. The extrapolation frequency is 12/min by default and configurable by users.

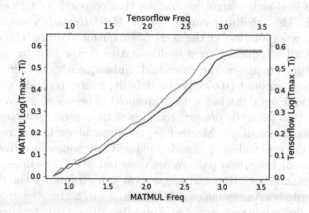

Fig. 4. The linear relationship between CPU frequency and logarithmic delta temperature of two benchmarks. The blue curve represents MATMUL and the orange curve represents the image recognition application. The plateaus at the right side of curves are caused by CPU hardware temperature throttling. (Color figure online)

2.2   Operating Modes

In the testing phase of Sparta, we identified two major problems in the decision plane. First, the extrapolation from linear regression oftentimes gets stuck at a local minimum. Thus, the determined CPU frequency is frequently lower than the ideal one, which leaves computational resources idle during execution. Second, the response time to correct the CPU from overheating is longer than expected when CPU temperature surpasses the threshold. To solve these two problems, we construct three operating modes for Sparta: Annealing, AIMD, and Hybrid.

Annealing is a probabilistic algorithm that leverages the epsilon-greedy strategy that balances exploration and exploitation by choosing randomly. In this mode, Sparta scheduler picks a value(P) in the range [0, 1] uniformly at random and compares it with ϵ/K, where ϵ is a probability of taking random actions (0.5 by default) and K is the number of extrapolation decision plane has made. The scheduler assigns a random CPU frequency when P is greater, whereas it keeps the extrapolated frequency when P is less than ϵ/K. With a decreasing probability of ϵ/K as the application proceeds, scheduler stabilizes and chooses to exploit what it has learned so far. When the ambient temperature or the execution pattern shifts dramatically, the scheduler resets the ϵ/K that allows more random exploration. This mode effectively addresses the problem of CPU frequency stuck at a local minimum and expedites the execution of machine learning applications under temperature threshold.

AIMD is a feedback control mechanism that responds to CPU temperature anomaly faster. The scheduler configures the CPU frequency according to the historical data extrapolation at the start of execution. During the execution, it decreases the CPU frequency by a multiplicative factor (0.5 by default) when CPU temperature surpasses the threshold. Subsequently, it increases the frequency by a fixed amount (0.07 GHz by default) every iteration until the CPU temperature stabilizes right below the threshold. The decision plane turns into hibernation at this point to prevent redundant tuning on CPU frequency that leads to inefficient execution. Meanwhile, the data plane keeps monitoring the CPU temperature and wakes up decision plane if any anomalies caused by ambient temperature or execution pattern are detected. AIMD reduces the response time to temperature deviation and keeps most samples under the threshold.

Hybrid combines Annealing and AIMD modes to address each other's disadvantage: if the probabilistic actions in Annealing drive CPU temperature above threshold, AIMD brings the anomaly back to normal fast; when AIMD settles at a local minimum of CPU frequency and leaves resources idle, Annealing boosts the execution by assigning a random CPU frequency. This way, Hybrid mode provides a complement to accelerate the machine learning execution while keeping the CPU temperature under threshold.

3   Evaluation

Based on the fact that most resource-demanding programs on edge cloud in our Sedgwick Natural Reserve settings are machine learning applications, in this section, we empirically evaluate Sparta's performance in a series of experiments on six benchmarks, ranging from image recognition, natural language processing to random forest and time series prediction, which are implemented based on Tensorflow and executed through Sparta's actuator interface. We first overview the machine learning benchmarks that we consider and our experimental methodology. We then present our results.

3.1   Machine Learning Benchmarks

To comprehensively evaluate the efficacy and efficiency of Sparta, we implemented 6 machine learning benchmarks, which consist of four categories: image recognition, natural language processing, ensemble learning and time series analysis. We aim to test Sparta on a variety of machine learning applications that represent different execution patterns.

WTB_Train is an image recognition application that we use as a benchmark to train a convolutional neural network (CNN) [8] based on ResNet50 [9]. The training dataset contains animal images from a wildlife monitoring system called" Where's The Bear" (WTB) [10]. "Where's The Bear" is an end-to-end distributed data acquisition and analytical system that automatically analyzes camera trap images collected by cameras sited at the Sedgwick Natural Reserve [2] in Santa Barbara County, California. In total, there are five classes that we consider: Bear, Coyote, Deer, Bird, and Empty, by which we label images for training tasks. We also up-sampled minority classes using the Keras Image Data Generator [11], since the class size is unbalanced due to the frequency of animal occurrences. Doing so ensures that the classification model is not biased. We resized every image in the dataset to 1920×1080, and for each class, the dataset contains 60 images used to train the CNN model. Once the training is complete, the application stores this model in hdf5 format in object storage.

The WTB_Train application has a cold start at the beginning of the execution since it loads a pre-trained neural network model and training datasets. Once it completes loading, the entire training process has relatively consistent CPU usage and temperature.

WTB_Inf inferences the type of wildlife in camera trap pictures based on the model trained by WTB_Train. It loads the trained hdf5 model at the beginning and, for each picture, it assigns probabilities to five classes we consider in the training dataset by Softmax function. In each experiment, we assign 20 pictures for WTB_Inf to inference. In terms of the execution pattern, WTB_Inf runs in short bursts as opposed to WTB_Train. Therefore, the CPU usage and temperature fluctuate dramatically throughout the execution of this benchmark.

MNIST is a dataset containing grayscale pictures of handwritten digits, in which it has 60,000 examples as the training set and 10,000 examples as the testing set. Based on the dataset, we train a 2-layer convolutional neural network [12] and test its accuracy in the third application. In contrast to WTB benchmarks, the size of pictures is smaller (28×28) and the model is simplified in MNIST.

BiLSTM is a sentiment analysis application based on a dataset of the Internet Movie Database (IMDB) movie reviews. It consists of 25,000 sequences each for training and testing. The model is constructed as a bidirectional LSTM with a classification layer using the sigmoid activation function. We train the model by the training dataset and validate its performance in classifying sentiment by the testing dataset. Since it has a large dataset and a complex model, the execution pattern is long-running and consistent in CPU usage and temperature.

Decision_Forest is an implementation of deep neural decision forests [13] that classifies high-earning individuals from the pool. The benchmark leverages the United States Census Income Dataset [14] that has 48,843 instances with 14 features, including age, education, occupation, etc. The dataset is split up that the training part has 32,561 instances and the testing part has 16,282 instances. The application has three phases: it firstly processes the dataset by encoding input features. Then, it trains a deep neural decision tree model. Based on that, the application trains a neural decision forest model consists of a set of neural decision trees. Therefore, the usage and temperature of CPU increasingly grow throughout the process.

Time_Series is a time series prediction application built on the climate data recorded by the Max Planck Institute for Biogeochemistry [15]. The dataset has 14 features such as temperature, pressure, humidity, etc. and the sampling frequency is 10 min. The time frame of the dataset ranges from Jan. 10th, 2009 to Dec. 31st, 2016. The application uses 300,693 rows to train a single-layer LSTM model, by which we can predict outdoor temperature in next 72 timestamps (12 h) given the samples in the past 720 timestamps (120 h). By this benchmark, we intend to evaluate Sparta on an application with a lightweight model and a large dataset.

3.2   Experimental Setup

Each edge cloud node used in the experiments is an Intel NUC [16] (6i7KYK) with two Intel Core i7-6770HQ 4-core processors (6M Cache, 2.60 GHz) and 32 GB of DDR4-2133+ RAM connected via two channels. We use dynamic voltage and frequency scaling (DVFS) to control the frequency of CPU from 0.8 GHz to 3.5 GHz.

To simulate the natural temperature in Sedgwick natural reserve, we create three thermal environments in an isolated cooler that represent cold, neutral, and hot ambient temperature. In the cold scenario, the ambient temperature is 2.64 °C and the CPU of NUC runs under 40 °C in idle status. In the neutral scenario, the CPU of NUC starts at 51 °C under the ambient temperature of 23.9 °C. The hot scenario increases the ambient and CPU temperature to 43.8 °C and 68 °C respectively.

There are two goals of the Sparta scheduler: the first is to limit the CPU temperature under the threshold; the second is to accelerate tasks without overheating the edge cloud. To evaluate these two objectives, we execute 6 machine learning benchmarks under 3 modes of Sparta scheduler. In each experiment, Sparta takes inputs of task program, corresponding workload dataset and a threshold temperature. To keep the comparison consistent across 3 thermal environments, we use 75 °C as the threshold temperature for all experiments (Fig. 5).

Fig. 5. Three thermal environments in the experiment

In 3 modes of Sparta, we execute each machine learning benchmark repeatedly 100 times under 3 thermal environments (totally $3 \times 3 \times 6 \times 100 = 5400$ executions) and report relevant metrics, both mean and standard deviation, to compare the efficacy and efficiency among Annealing, AIMD, and Hybrid modes.

3.3   Application Efficacy

We first measure the stabilization time for six benchmarks. We define stabilization time as the elapsed time from the start to the point all CPU temperatures in the sampling time window are within $[T_s - T_d, T_s]$, where T_s is the threshold and T_d is a slack variable (3 °C by default). During each of the 10 consecutive executions (1 epoch) of benchmarks, we record the duration when the Sparta scheduler stabilizes the CPU temperature according to the threshold. As shown in the first part of Table 1, we report the mean and stdev of stabilization time for each benchmark in 3 modes. Hybrid mode uses less time to stabilize CPU temperature than Annealing and AIMD in all six benchmarks. It performs even better in WTB_Inf benchmark that has a short burst execution pattern and volatile CPU temperature.

As the second part of Table 1 presents the result in the thermal dimension, Hybrid mode also uses less time to stabilize CPU temperature across all 3 thermal environments, comparing to Annealing and AIMD. Averagely, Hybrid mode uses 43.61 s in the stabilization phase, in contrast to 61.16 s in Annealing and 65.9 s in AIMD. Hybrid mode's performance is even better in the hot scenario, which is the key use case for edge devices to prevent overheating in Sedgwick natural reserve.

We next empirically evaluate the execution time of six benchmarks by the Sparta scheduler. In the first part of Table 2, we report the mean and stdev of execution time for each benchmark under 3 modes. On average, the Hybrid mode completes the task of each benchmark faster than Annealing and AIMD. Given the stdev and degree of freedom, we also run student t-test among 3 modes for each benchmark and confirm that the execution time by Hybrid is smaller than Annealing and AIMD with a statistical significance level of 5%. Table 2 also indicates the speedup of Hybrid over Annealing and AIMD, ranging from 1.04x to 1.32x.

Table 1. The mean and stdev of **stabilization time** in seconds for 6 machine learning benchmarks in 3 Sparta modes. Compared to Annealing and AIMD, Hybrid mode uses less time to stabilize CPU temperature across all benchmarks and all thermal scenarios.

	WTB train	WTB Inf	MNIST	BiLSTM	Decision forest	Time series
Annealing	53.79 (30.1)	50.7 (21.1)	62.02 (32.2)	69.02 (33.8)	59.13 (31.9)	72.31 (28.8)
AIMD	61.73 (24.9)	63.26 (25.0)	58.91 (14.0)	59.9 (11.2)	78.17 (30.7)	73.41 (28.9)
Hybrid	38.59 (26.11)	23.24 (17.33)	38.66 (22.17)	52.83 (20.6)	55.46 (25.5)	52.91 (29.8)

	Neutral	Cold	Hot	Average
Annealing	68.15	67.27	48.07	61.16
AIMD	63.10	77.40	57.20	65.90
Hybrid	43.03	52.43	35.39	43.61

The second part of Table 2 demonstrates the average execution time in 3 thermal scenarios. On average, Hybrid mode completes the task in 126.61 s, in comparison with 146.09 s by Annealing and 147.46 s by AIMD. Hybrid mode provides 1.16x and 1.14x speedup respectively over Annealing and AIMD. These results show that Sparta in Hybrid mode efficiently executes more workloads than Annealing and AIMD mode under the same temperature threshold.

To investigate the error from the sampling temperature and threshold, we next evaluate the Root Mean Square Error (RMSE) of all temperature samples in the executions. We define $RMSE = \sqrt{\frac{1}{n} \sum_{i=1}^{n} (T_i - \hat{T})^2}$, where T_i is a sample of CPU temperature, $\hat{T}$ is the temperature threshold and n is the number of temperature samples. In Table 3, we display the mean and stdev of RMSE of all CPU temperature samples. The RMSE of Hybrid mode is the least across all six benchmarks among the other two modes. Hybrid mode also has the lowest

Table 2. The mean and stdev of **execution time** in seconds for 6 machine learning benchmarks in 3 modes of Sparta. Compared to Annealing and AIMD, Hybrid mode uses less time to complete tasks across all benchmarks and all thermal scenarios.

	WTB train	WTB Inf	MNIST	BiLSTM	Decision forest	Time series
Annealing	374.67 (9.8)	60.94 (3.9)	39.85 (2.9)	222.34 (3.5)	48.21 (3.6)	130.65 (7.6)
Speedup	1.17x	1.10x	1.21x	1.04x	1.15x	1.32x
AIMD	393.55 (5.8)	64.32 (3.9)	36.51 (4.3)	234.92 (5.2)	45.38 (2.2)	110.06 (6.2)
Speedup	1.22x	1.16x	1.13x	1.10x	1.09x	1.11x
Hybrid	318.55 (4.2)	55.31 (3.2)	32.53 (2.3)	212.91 (2.6)	41.56 (4.4)	98.78 (7.2)

	Neutral	Cold	Hot	Average
Annealing	145.72	116.14	176.42	146.09
Speedup	1.17x	1.06x	1.26x	1.16x
AIMD	134.67	122.28	185.42	147.46
Speedup	1.07x	1.15x	1.18x	1.14x
Hybrid	124.86	107.68	147.28	126.61

Table 3. The mean and stdev of **RMSE** of all temperature samples for 6 benchmarks in 3 modes of Sparta. Compared to Annealing and AIMD, Hybrid mode has less RSME to threshold temperature across all benchmarks and all thermal scenarios.

	WTB train	WTB Inf	MNIST	BiLSTM	Decision forest	Time series
Annealing	5.04 (1.0)	7.88 (1.7)	9.22 (0.8)	5.07 (1.3)	9.91 (1.5)	9.63 (2.4)
AIMD	4.39 (0.6)	6.24 (0.9)	8.35 (1.0)	5.81 (2.1)	9.95 (1.6)	8.67 (3.1)
Hybrid	4.32 (0.6)	5.79 (1.2)	6.11 (1.8)	4.90 (1.2)	9.48 (2.4)	7.25 (3.0)

	Neutral	Cold	Hot	Average
Annealing	7.12	9.59	6.67	7.79
AIMD	5.69	9.39	5.79	6.96
Hybrid	4.92	9.10	4.99	6.34

RMSE in all three thermal scenarios. On average, Hybrid has 6.34 as RMSE for all temperature samples from the threshold.

Lastly, we report the percentage of samples below threshold temperature in six benchmarks. The first part of Table 4 manifests the mean and stdev of PTBT (Percentage of Temperature Below Threshold) for six benchmarks. Because Annealing mode uses a probabilistic algorithm, it results in the lowest PTBT metric among three modes. Since AIMD mode multiplicatively decreases the CPU frequency whenever a temperature over the threshold is detected, it has the highest PTBT metrics in all six benchmarks. Combined with Annealing and AIMD, the PTBT of Hybrid mode is between the other two modes. This relationship holds for all three thermal scenarios, as depicted in the second part of Table 4. Hybrid mode maintains 94.4% of all temperature samples below the threshold. Thus, we consider the above results strong proofs of Sparta's efficacy in preventing overheating of edge devices and executing a variety of tasks as efficiently as possible.

Table 4. The mean and stdev of **PTBT** (Percentage of Temperature Below Threshold) for 6 benchmarks in 3 modes of Sparta. Due to their inherent algorithm, Annealing has the lowest PTBT value and AIMD has the highest, whereas the Hybrid mode has the PTBT value in-between across all benchmarks and all thermal scenarios.

	WTB train	WTB Inf	MNIST	BiLSTM	Decision forest	Time series
Annealing	71.8% (0.05)	83.0% (0.14)	83.4% (0.09)	72.6% (0.10)	84.3% (0.07)	91.0% (0.13)
AIMD	97.2% (0.07)	99.7% (0.01)	98.0% (0.08)	99.6% (0.09)	98.7% (0.04)	99.5% (0.25)
Hybrid	93.0% (0.11)	95.2% (0.14)	92.7% (0.07)	97.2% (0.23)	91.1% (0.10)	96.9% (0.17)

	Neutral	Cold	Hot	Average
Annealing	88.3%	79.7%	75.1%	81.1%
AIMD	99.7%	98.6%	98.2%	98.8%
ybrid	98.1%	92.29%	92.7%	94.4%

4 Related Work

As related work, we consider recent advances in edge cloud's energy consumption and power management. [17] proposes computational sprinting which is a class of mechanisms that supplies additional power on processors for short duration to improve performance. It also introduces phase change materials onto processors to absorb additional heat primarily concerning the performance. Thrifty-Edge [18] presents a resource-efficient edge computing paradigm that consists of an offloading mechanism based on delay-aware task graph partition and a virtual machine selection method. To augment existing resources, [19] manifests a dynamic fog computing framework that schedules computing tasks to Citizen Fog (CF) with the highest computational ability. Different from the above systems, Sparta focuses on preventing CPU overheating caused by ambient temperature and program execution patterns on edge cloud deployed in natural conditions.

By offering distributed, reliable, and low-latency machine learning services, edge-based ML as a fast-growing area has a great appeal both for AI and system research community. Thus, we also consider the cutting-edge development in machine learning based on edge cloud. [20] explores the building blocks and principles of wireless intelligence at edge networks concerning latency reduction, reliability guarantees, scalability enhancement, and privacy constraints. [21] provides a comprehensive survey of techniques in the scope of machine learning system at the network edge, including distributed training and inference, real-time video analytics and speech recognition, autonomous vehicles and smart cities, etc. [22] presents an approach to estimate the performance of ML application on edge cloud and to load appropriate computing resources for an edge-based application. The above work provide guiding principles and examples for Sparta and serve as one of the key motivations for our work.

5 Conclusion

In this paper, we propose a heat budget-based scheduling framework, called Sparta, aiming to prevent edge cloud CPU overheating in executing machine learning applications. Sparta's scheduler integrates three components – data plane, decision plane, and control plane: Decision plane extrapolates the initial CPU frequency from historical benchmark data and dynamically adjusts it based on real-time data monitored by data plane, while control plane modified the CPU frequency via DVFS throughout the execution. Sparta strives to accelerate the execution of applications without sacrificing the CPU overheating protection.

We present the design principles and implementation details of Sparta's components and operating modes that address the drawback we encounter in the testing phase. Our empirical evaluation demonstrates Sparta effectively protects CPU from overheating, putting **94.4%** temperature samples under the threshold in Hybrid mode. In the meantime, it speeds six benchmarks' execution up to **1.04x - 1.32x** in all three thermal environments compared to Annealing and AIMD.

As part of future work, we plan to investigate using non-uniform distributions in generating random values for exploration in Annealing mode that potentially improves the PTBT metrics. We also plan to extend the deployment of Sparta at edge cloud clusters and investigate its performance in the distributed execution of training and inference process.

Acknowledgment. This work has been supported in part by NSF (CNS-2107101, CNS-1703560, CCF-1539586, ACI-1541215), ONR NEEC (N00174-16-C-0020), and the AWS Cloud Credits for Research program. This work was performed in part at the University of California Natural Reserve System Sedgwick Reserve DOI: 10.21973/N3C08R.

References

1. Hassan, N., Gillani, S., Ahmed, E., Yaqoob, I., Imran, M.: The role of edge computing in internet of things. IEEE Commun. Mag. **56**(11), 110–115 (2018). https://doi.org/10.1109/MCOM.2018.1700906
2. Sedgwick Natural Reserve. https://sedgwick.nrs.ucsb.edu. Accessed 30 Apr 2021
3. https://www.intel.com/content/www/us/en/support/articles/000005597/processors.html . Accessed 30 Apr 2021
4. Liu, Y., Yang, H., Dick, R.P., Wang, H., Shang, L.: Thermal vs energy optimization for DVFs-enabled processors in embedded systems. In: 8th International Symposium on Quality Electronic Design (ISQED'07), pp. 204–209. IEEE (2007)
5. Wang, L., Von Laszewski, G., Dayal, J., Wang, F.: Towards energy aware scheduling for precedence constrained parallel tasks in a cluster with DVFS. In: 2010 10th IEEE/ACM International Conference on Cluster, Cloud and Grid Computing, pp. 368–377. IEEE (2010)
6. https://github.com/lm-sensors/lm-sensors. Accessed 30 Apr 2021
7. https://www.tensorflow.org/. Accessed 30 Apr 2021
8. LeCun, Y., Bengio, Y.: Convolutional Networks for Images, Speech, and Time Series. The Handbook of Brain Theory and Neural Networks, pp. 255–258. MIT Press, Cambridge (1998)
9. He, K., Zhang, X., Ren, S., Sun, J.: Deep residual learning for image recognition. In: Proceedings of the IEEE Conference on Computer Vision and Pattern Recognition, pp. 770–778 (2016)
10. Elias, A.R., Golubovic, N., Krintz, C., Wolski, R.: Where's the bear? Automating wildlife image processing using IoT and edge cloud systems. In: 2017 IEEE/ACM Second International Conference on Internet-of-Things Design and Implementation (IoTDI), pp. 247–258 (2017)
11. Keras Image Data Generator. https://keras.io/preprocessing/image/#imagedatagenerator-class. Accessed 30 Apr 2021
12. LeCun, Y., Bottou, L., Bengio, Y., Haffner, P.: Gradient-based learning applied to document recognition. Proc. IEEE **86**(11), 2278–2324 (1998)
13. Kontschieder, P., Fiterau, M., Criminisi, A., Bulò, S.R.: Deep neural decision forests. In: 2015 IEEE International Conference on Computer Vision (ICCV), pp. 1467–1475 (2015). https://doi.org/10.1109/ICCV.2015.172
14. https://archive.ics.uci.edu/ml/datasets/census+income. Accessed 30 Apr 2021
15. https://www.bgc-jena.mpg.de/wetter/. Accessed 30 Apr 2021

16. https://www.intel.com/content/www/us/en/products/boards-kits/nuc.html . Accessed 30 Apr 2021
17. Zahedi, S.M., Fan, S., Faw, M., Cole, E., Lee, B.C.: Computational sprinting: architecture, dynamics, and strategies. ACM Trans. Comput. Syst. **34**(4), 26 (2017). https://doi.org/10.1145/3014428. Article 12
18. Chen, X., Shi, Q., Yang, L., Xu, J.: ThriftyEdge: resource-efficient edge computing for intelligent IoT applications. IEEE Netw. **32**(1), 61–65 (2018). https://doi.org/10.1109/MNET.2018.1700145
19. Hossain, M.R., et al.: A scheduling-based dynamic fog computing framework for augmenting resource utilization. Simul. Model. Pract. Theory **111**, 102336 (2021). https://doi.org/10.1016/j.simpat.2021.102336. ISSN 1569–190X
20. Park, J., Samarakoon, S., Bennis, M., Debbah, M.: Wireless network intelligence at the edge. Proc. IEEE **107**, 2204–2239 (2019). https://doi.org/10.1109/JPROC.2019.2941458
21. Sarwar Murshed, M.G., Murphy, C.,Hou, D.,Khan, N., Ananthanarayanan, G., Hussain, F.: Machine Learning at the Network Edge, A Survey (2019)
22. Cruz, B.D., Paul, A.K., Song, Z., Tilevich, E.: Stargazer: a deep learning approach for estimating the performance of edge-based clustering applications. In: 2020 IEEE International Conference on Smart Data Services (SMDS), pp. 9–17 (2020). https://doi.org/10.1109/SMDS49396.2020.00009

Integrated 5G MEC System and Its Application in Intelligent Video Analytics

Han Wang[1,2,3,4]($\boxtimes$), Chunxiao Xing[1,2], and Liang-Jie Zhang[3,4]

[1] Research Institute of Information Technology, Beijing National Research Center for Information Science and Technology, Tsinghua University, Beijing 100084, China
[2] Department of Computer Science and Technology, Institute of Internet Industry, Tsinghua University, Beijing 100084, China
[3] National Engineering Research Center for Supporting Software of Enterprise Internet Services, Shenzhen 518057, China
[4] Kingdee Research, Kingdee International Software Group Company Limited, Shenzhen 518057, China

Abstract. Along with commercial use globally, 5G system is getting more and more attention from various vertical industries for its excellent network capabilities, where one of the key enabling technologies is Multi-access Edge Computing (MEC). MEC is a network solution that provides services and functions required by users on the nearby edge computing platform, ensuring low latency, high stability and sufficient capability, and hence is more suitable for real-time scenarios compared to the conventional fully central cloud-based paradigm. The integrated 5G MEC system brings the connectivity, computing and applications together in a converged ecosystem that will enable differentiated service innovations and empower intelligent transformation of vertical industries. In this paper, we introduce the principle and architecture of the integrated 5G MEC system, and propose an innovative application of 5G MEC based intelligent video analytics. By performing an on-site experiment, we validate the feasibility and performance of the proposed scheme, and then discuss the features and applicable scopes between edge-based and conventional cloud-based paradigms.

Keywords: 5G · MEC · Intelligent video analytics

1 Introduction

The key features of the 5G system are summarized as enhanced Mobile Broad-Band (eMBB), ultra-Reliable and Low-Latency Communications (uRLLC), and massive Machine Type Communications (mMTC) [1]. In the 5G era, more and more new applications, such as 4K/8K high definition video, Augmented Reality (AR) and Virtual Reality (VR), place higher requirements on network latency and bandwidth. Multi-access Edge Computing (MEC) [2] is acknowledged as one of the key enabling technologies to achieve such requirements.

This work is supported by National Key R&D Program of China (2020AAA0109603).

L.-J. Zhang (Ed.): EDGE 2021, LNCS 12990, pp. 35–49, 2022.
https://doi.org/10.1007/978-3-030-96504-4_3

MEC is a distributed computing platform embedded at the edge of the network, offering Infrastructure-as-a-Service (IaaS) and Platform-as-a-Service (PaaS) similar to the conventional cloud computing. MEC can provide low latency and high bandwidth services to nearby users to meet their critical needs in agile connection, real-time business, data optimization, application intelligence, security and privacy protection. The 5G system provides the network infrastructure for deploying MEC with flexible user plane function and network function opening. The integrated 5G MEC system [3,4] brings computing platform and 5G core networks to the edge of the network, introducing new traffic models and deployment models. The new paradigm of "5G+MEC" is essential to enable various industrial applications and empowering intelligent transformation of vertical industries.

One of the most representative applications is 5G MEC based intelligent video analytics. Nowadays, intelligent video applications [5–8], from face recognition to content understanding, are widely used to interpret and understand the visual world. The general workflow of intelligent video analytics follows the steps of "capture-transmit-process-analyze" separately: the real-time video stream is captured by a generic camera, and then transmitted to a remote cloud computing platform to process and analyze. However, the above workflow is usually deployed on a conventional central cloud platform, suffering the bottlenecks of bandwidth, delay and security, which limits the application fields of intelligent video analytics. Fortunately, with the rapid development of integrated 5G MEC system, the real-time video stream can be transmitted to the nearby MEC to process and analyze via 5G network. The solution of 5G MEC based intelligent video system supports flexible access to the nearby edge server with high bandwidth and low latency, saving massive volume of video data traffic, and ensuring security of video processing and analyzing. By leveraging the integrated 5G MEC system, the application fields of intelligent video analytics can be extended to a wider range of scenarios.

This paper introduces the integrated 5G MEC system and the corresponding intelligent video application. The rest of this paper is organized as follows. In Sect. 2, we introduce the logical and physical architecture of 5G network, MEC and the integrated system respectively. In Sect. 3, we propose a practical 5G MEC based intelligent video system, validate the feasibility and performance by conducting an on-site experiment, and then compare the features and applicable scopes between edge-based and conventional cloud-based paradigms. At last, the paper is concluded in Sect. 4.

2   Integrated 5G MEC System

The 5G system is a key future target environment for MEC deployments. The 3rd Generation Partnership Project (3GPP) defines specifications of 5G system architecture [9], which leverage the service based interactions between different network functions to align system operations with Network Function Virtualization (NFV) and Software Defined Networking (SDN) paradigms. The similar characteristics above are shared by the MEC specifications [10], which are defined by the European Telecommunications Standards Institute (ETSI). In addition, 3GPP specifications define the enablers for edge computing, allowing that 5G and MEC interact collaboratively in traffic routing and policy control. Integrating the above 5G technical enablers with MEC features can formulate a powerful edge computing environment.

In this section, we introduce architectures of the 3GPP 5G system and the ETSI MEC system respectively, and then discuss the logical and physical frameworks of the integrated 5G MEC system.

2.1 5G System Architecture

The 5G system is designed for a wide range of use cases, from high-speed data transmission, ultra-low latency round-trip control, to massive IoT connection. In order to support all the use cases with the same and common architecture, both Radio Access Network (RAN) and Core Network (CN) are significantly changed in the design philosophy of "Cloud Native".

The 3GPP defines the specification of Service Based Architecture (SBA) [9] for 5G System, illustrated in Fig. 1, to support data connectivity and services enabling deployments with NFV and SDN. With the SBA, there are Virtual Network Functions (VNFs) that consume services and those that produce services. Any VNF can offer one or more services via its corresponding interfaces. The key principle of SBA can be summarized as Control Plane and User Plane Separation (CUPS), which achieves independent scalability, evolution and flexible deployments.

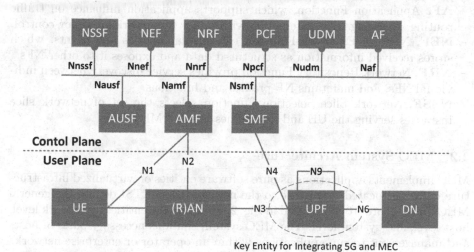

Key Entity for Integrating 5G and MEC

Fig. 1. Service based architecture for 5G system

User Plane. The User Plane (UP) carries the network user traffic data, mainly including:

- **UE** User Equipment is any device used by an end user such as a smart phone or other mobile devices equipped with a 5G network adapter.
- **RAN** Radio Access Network is responsible for connecting UEs to CN through wireless antennas of radio base stations.
- **UPF** User Plane Function is responsible for packet handling and forwarding, mobility anchor, and Internet Protocol (IP) anchor towards the Internet, which is the key entity of 5G MEC integration.
- **DN** Data Network provides operator services, Internet access or 3rd party services.

Control Plane. The Control Plane (CP) carries the system traffic signaling, and supports the functions of establishing and maintaining UP. Network Functions (NFs) of CP mainly includes:

- **AUSF.** AUthentication Server Function authenticates UEs and stores authentication keys.
- **AMF.** Access and mobility Management Function manages UE registration and authentication (via AUSF) and identification (via UDM) and mobility. It also terminates non-access stratum signaling.
- **SMF.** Session Management Function establishes and manages sessions. It also selects and controls UPF and handles paging.
- **PCF.** Policy Control Function provides policy rules to CP functions.
- **UDM.** Unified Data Management stores subscriber data and profiles, and generates the authentication vector.
- **AF.** Application Function, which supports application influence on traffic routing, accessing NEF, interaction with policy framework for policy control.
- **NEF.** Network Exposure Function exposes capabilities and events, which stores received information as structured data and exposes it to other NFs.
- **NRF.** Network Repository Function provides service discovery between individual NFs, and maintains NF profiles and functions.
- **NSSF.** Network Slice Selection Function selects the set of network slice instances serving the UE and determines which AMF to use.

2.2   MEC System Architecture

MEC implements applications as pure software entities on virtualized infrastructure, which is located in or close to the network edge. ETSI defines the general MEC architecture [10] illustrated in Fig. 2, grouping the entities as network level, host level, and system level. The MEC system contains necessary parts of hosts and management to run applications within an operator or enterprise network.

Network Level. The MEC architecture takes various kinds of network access technologies (e.g. 3GPP cellular, Ethernet, Wi-Fi, etc.) into account to achieve the multiple accessibility of the edge system.

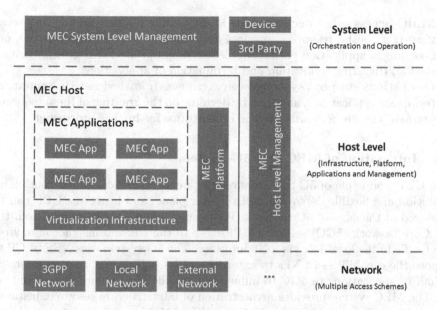

Fig. 2. MEC architecture

Host Level. The host level of MEC architecture includes MEC hosts and the MEC host level management.

- **MEC host** is an entity, consisting of a virtualization infrastructure and a MEC platform, for running MEC applications.
  - **Virtualization infrastructure** provides virtualized resources of compute, storage and network for applications.
  - **MEC platform (MEP)** is the essential function set required to run applications on the above infrastructure and enable them to provide and consume MEC services.
  - **MEC applications** are instantiated on MEC host infrastructure, based on configuration or requests validated by MEC management.
- **MEC host level management** manages specific functions of particular MEC host and its corresponding applications.
  - **MEC platform manager (MEPM)** is responsible for managing application life cycles, rules and requirements, and providing element management functions to MEP.
  - **Virtualization infrastructure manager** is responsible for allocating, managing and releasing virtualized resources, rapid application provisioning, performing application relocation, collecting and reporting performance and fault information about the resources.

System Level. The MEC system level management includes the core component of orchestrator to overview the complete MEC system, and a corresponding operations support system.

- **Multi-access edge orchestrator** is responsible for maintaining an overall view (e.g., hosts, resources, services and topology) of the MEC system, onboarding of application packages, selecting appropriate MEC host for instantiation, triggering, relocation and termination of applications.
- **Operations support system** receives requests from devices to instantiate or terminate applications, and then by deciding on the granting of these requests, granted ones are forwarded to the orchestrator for further processing.

2.3   Integration of MEC and 5G System

The CUPS principle of 5G SBA ensures the independent scalability, continuous evolution and flexible deployment of the user plane, and hence the UPF can be deployed at the edge of 5G network. When supporting an edge application, the 5G Core network (5GC) selects a UPF close to the UE and instruct it to steer the traffic to the local DN via a N6 interface. The 5G system uses NEF of CP to expose the capabilities of NFs to external entities, which may send requests on behalf of applications to 5GC to influence on traffic routing and policy control.

The MEC system provides orchestration of infrastructure resource, instantiation and configuration for applications. When MEC system is integrated into 5G networks, it is essential for applications to expose the traffic steering control information to the 5G network. Since applications are managed and orchestrated by MEC system, MEC is reasonable to provide the support of 5GC-to-MEC interaction for applications. MEC management components are divided into system level and host level, where the former could be centralized deployed so as to facilitate communications with external entities.

Figure 3 illustrates a typical integrated architecture [3,4] of MEC and 5G System. In this framework, both of system level MEC orchestrator and host level MEC platform are acting as AFs which can interact with NEF or other 5G NFs when necessary. The MEC hosts are usually deployed as the role of DN of the 5G system, which is enabled by flexibility in locating the UPF. As a CN function, NEF is a system level entity usually deployed centrally together with similar NFs. Also, an instance of NEF can be flexibly deployed in the edge to ensure low latency and high throughput service access from a MEC host.

MEC hosts are logically deployed in the edge or central DN, acting as UPF which steers the UP traffic towards the targeted MEC applications in the DN. However, the physical locations of the DN and UPF are a choice of the network operator by considering various of technical and business aspects, such as available site facilities, supported applications and corresponding requirements, measured or estimated user work load etc. As an operation orchestrator of MEC hosts and applications, the MEC management system can dynamically determine where to deploy MEC applications. Actually, the MEC system can be flexibly deployed in different locations from near the base station to the central data center, as demonstrated in Fig. 4, where the common deployment principle is that UPF should be deployed and used to steer data traffic towards the targeted MEC applications.

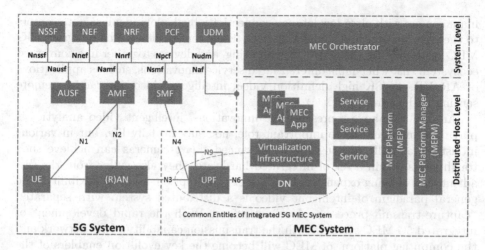

Fig. 3. Integration of MEC and 5G system

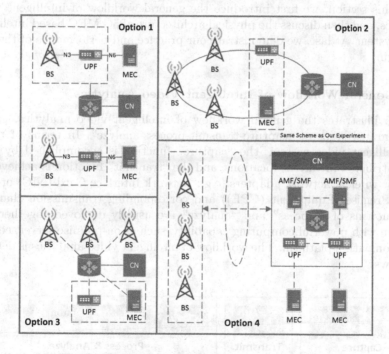

Fig. 4. Physical deployment of 5G MEC system

3   5G MEC Based Intelligent Video Analytics

Along with the commercial use globally, the 5G network has been demonstrated the transmission capacity of enhanced mobile broadband and fixed wireless access services to user equipment. MEC enables real-time data processing and management with ultra-low latency connectivity by deploying micro data centers to the network edge and connecting back to the central cloud. The integrated 5G MEC system brings the network, computing, and devices together in a converged ecosystem that will enable differentiated service innovations, such as applications of AR/VR, 4K/8K high definition video, intelligent video, interactive remote sensing and control.

Among the above representative innovations, intelligent video analytics is playing a more and more important role, not only in daily life, but in various industries as well. Although some advanced smart cameras can achieve such tough tasks within a set of integrated hardware, they also suffer from the disadvantages of being expensive, high power consumption, and low flexibility. The general paradigm of intelligent video is a distributed system with separated "capture-transmit-process-analyze" workflow. With the rapid development of integrated 5G MEC system, both the transmission capability of 5G network and the computing platform of MEC will become the key evolution enablers of the above distributed intelligent video system.

In this section, we first introduce the general workflow of intelligent video analytics, and then discuss the physical architecture of 5G MEC based intelligent video system. At last, we demonstrate our practice and performance of the new paradigm.

3.1   General Workflow of Intelligent Video Analytics

Figure 5 illustrates the general workflow of intelligent video analytics, following separated steps of "capture-transmit-process-analyze". In terms of physical intelligent video system, the "capture" function is accomplished by cameras distributed in various locations, and the "transmit" function is achieved by wired or wireless network adapters (e.g., Network Interface Card (NIC) or Customer Premises Equipment (CPE)) and corresponding transmission channels. The functions of "process" and "analyze" are usually deployed together in a platform with powerful computing capability, such as on-premise server, edge or cloud computing platform. The workflow of intelligent video analytics is detailed as follows.

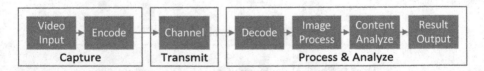

Fig. 5. General workflow of intelligent video analytics

Capture. The physical scene is captured by a camera as the real-time video source to be analyzed. The captured raw live video has a large bit rate, and hence needs to be compressed with a source-encoder (e.g., H.264 or H.265) to reduce the burden of network transmission. Optionally, if the source-encoded video stream needs to be transmitted over unreliable or noisy communication channel directly, a channel-encoder should be added after the source-encoder to increase information redundancy and control transmission error with the error correction code (e.g., Low-Density Parity-Check (LDPC)).

Transmit. The encoded video stream needs to be transmitted through a channel to a remote computing platform to process and analyze. The commonly used video transmission channel is IP based networks such as Ethernet, Wi-Fi and 4G/5G cellular network. The encoded video stream is segmented and packed into IP packages by the network adapter, and then transmitted through the channel sequentially with the help of live streaming protocols (e.g., Real-time Streaming Protocol (RTSP), Real-time Messaging Protocol (RTMP) and HTTP Live Streaming (HLS)).

Process and Analyze. When the IP packages arrive at the remote computing platform, the network adapter unpack and combine them to assemble the encoded video stream. The original raw live video is recovered from encoded stream by the decoder, and then extracted into images for further processing. Since the captured images may have defects in size, noise and effects, they need to be pre-processed by image scale, denoise and enhance techniques to facilitate subsequent content analysis. The core procedure of the workflow is analyzing video contents, such as detecting, classifying and recognizing objects, which are usually achieved by various Deep Neural Network (DNN) based artificial intelligence algorithms. At last, the analyzed results should be outputted to the screen with a overlay boundary box, and the video along with corresponding metadata also should be archived to the storage system.

3.2 5G MEC Based Intelligent Video System

China United Network Communications Group Co., Ltd. (i.e., China Unicom, one of the three major telecommunications operators in China) has officially launched the world's first large-scale commercial MEC network on April 29, 2020 [11]. In the past year, China Unicom's 5G MEC system has been applied to various fields, from industrial manufacturing, ports, mines, transportation, electric power, healthcare, to content creation, becoming the essential to enable various industrial applications and empower intelligent transformation of vertical industries.

Intelligent video analytics is one of the key techniques widely used in the above vertical fields. Most off-the-shelf solutions either rely on complex cameras with dedicated software leading to expensive costs, or fully centralized cloud computing leading to longer response time and huge bandwidth requirements from connected cameras. It has been seriously noticed that live video streams result in heavy load on both networks and centralized data centers for the actual processing of the video sources. In order to overcome the above problems, we collaborate with China Unicom together to explore, research and validate the implementation scheme of intelligent video analytics in the 5G MEC system.

China Unicom provides a complete end-to-end MEC experimental environment for developers to deploy and validate their proposed innovative applications. Figure 6 illustrates its detailed architecture which includes multi-access network, edge computing platform and multi-tier framework. The experimental environment offers multi-access network of 3G/4G/5G, NB-IoT, Wi-Fi and Ethernet for multiple kinds of UEs to connect to data centers. The edge computing platform is the MEC host, located in the edge or core network data center, which provides IaaS, PaaS and optional accelerating modules (e.g., Graphics Processing Unit (GPU), Field Programmable Gate Array (FPGA) or Application Specific Integrated Circuit (ASIC)) for the developers to deploy their applications. The multi-tier framework shares the same physical deployment and management as the commercial MEC system, ensuring that the functionality and performance of the proposed applications can be fully verified.

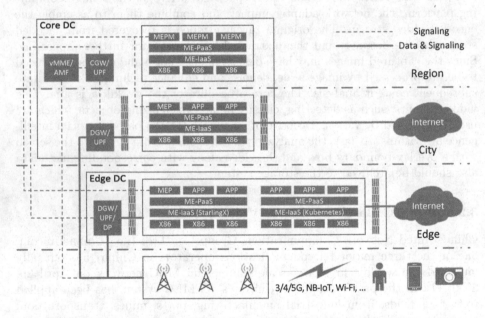

Fig. 6. System architecture of China Unicom's MEC experimental environment

Based on the above China Unicom's 5G MEC experimental environment, we develop a real-time mobile application of "Panoramic Object Detection", which is suitable for traffic condition recognition of self-driving cars, unmanned inspection of on-site environments, automatic annotation of panoramic maps, etc. The proposed application follows the general workflow of "capture-transmit-process-analyze", and the corresponding hardware deployment and software implementation schemes are illustrated in Fig. 7.

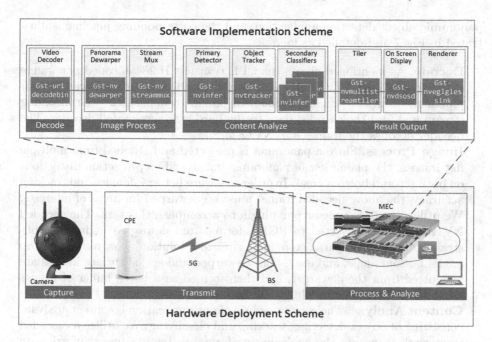

Fig. 7. System architecture of 5G MEC based panoramic object detection

Hardware Deployment Scheme. We utilize an "Insta360 Pro 2" panoramic camera as the live video source, which can not only capture the surrounding 360 degree scenes, but also encode the video with H.264 and stream it out with RTSP in real time. A "Huawei 5G CPE Pro", which is wired to the camera, is used for accessing the 5G wireless network and transmitting the IP packages of the video stream to the edge data center. Our panoramic object detection application is deployed on a MEC host server, which is equipped with quadruple NVIDIA T4 Tensor Core GPUs (i.e., universal deep learning accelerators), in the nearby edge data center. The detected panoramic video and system performance dashboard can be visited from a web browser, and the corresponding metadata are stored on the server as well.

Software Implementation Scheme. NVIDIA DeepStream [12] is a Software Development Kit (SDK) for intelligent video analytics applications and multi-sensor processing. Its key feature is the ability to bring DNN and other complex processing tasks into the streaming pipeline using hardware acceleration, allowing users to focus more on building DNN tasks rather than building end-to-end solutions from scratch. DeepStream is essentially a GStreamer [13] based plugin system which integrates NVIDIA technologies (such as TensorRT, cuDNN, CUDA, Video SDK, etc.) to develop intelligent video analytics applications in the form of pipelines. We utilize the NVIDIA DeepStream SDK to develop our panoramic object detection application, and the corresponding pipeline is illustrated in Fig. 7 and detailed as follows.

- **Decode.** As mentioned above, the CPE transmit H.264 encoded panoramic video frames over RTSP, and RTSP packetized data are received by our pipeline. We utilize `Gst-uridecodebin` plugin to depacketize the incoming stream and feed the encoded data to the hardware accelerated decoder. The decoder decodes the frames into NV12 format.
- **Image Process.** Since a panorama is projected and stitched from multiple flat images, the plain view of panoramic image suffers projection distortions on both top and bottom areas. In order to ensure better inference and tracking accuracy, the above decoded frames must be dewarped for areas of interests. We utilize the `Gst-nvdewarper` plugin to accomplish this task. The decoded NV12 data are converted to RGBA format and dewarped under the constraint of dewarping parameters (e.g., surface resolution, yaw, roll, pitch, top angle, bottom angle, and etc.). Four dewarped and scaled surface images are outputted from the dewarper, and then formed as a batch buffer of frames by the `Gst-nvstreammux` plugin for further analysis.
- **Content Analyze.** The core procedure of our application is content analysis, consisting of object detecting, tracking and classifying. We utilize a cascaded framework to ensure the analyzing performance by avoiding reinferring on the same objects in every frame. A `Gst-nvinfer` plugin performs as a primary detector to detect every objects from all of the input frames, and then each detected object is tagged with an Unique IDentifier (UID) by the following object tracker `Gst-nvtracker`. By caching the above output in a map with UID as the key, a group of `Gst-nvinfer` performs as secondary classifiers to classify the above tagged objects and extract structure information. The primary and secondary `Gst-nvinfer` plugins use the same pretrained "TrafficCamNet" ResNet DNN model to detect cars, persons, road signs and two-wheelers on the road, and output batched buffer of frames along with metadata of detected objects.
- **Result Output.** The above analyzed results of panoramic video should be outputted appropriately. We utilize the `Gst-nvmultistreamtiler` plugin to composite a 2D tile from batched buffers, and draw bounding boxes on the detected objects with `Gst-nvdsosd`. The `Gst-nveglglessink` plugin renders the above tagged frames into video stream, which is then streamed out by a GStreamer RTSP server in real time to facilitate playback in a web browser. Moreover, both the rendered video and the corresponding metadata are archived to the storage system for further use.

3.3   Experimental Results

An actual scenario of "traffic condition recognition" is selected to validate the feasibility and performance of our proposed 5G MEC based panoramic object detection. Although our solution supports on-vehicle capture and transmission on the move, we choose to conduct the experiment at a fixed location due to the complexity of vehicle modification and equipment installation.

We mount the "Insta360 Pro 2" and "Huawei 5G CPE Pro" together on a tripod and place it at an intersection. The panoramic camera captures the surrounding 360° scenes of the intersection, and then encodes and streams the live video out to the CPE. Through China Unicom's 5G RAN, the received IP packages of the live video stream are transmitted to a nearby (within 2 km) MEC data center by the CPE. Our software analyzes the received panoramic video on the MEC host, and then pushes the detected result (i.e., the original video along with overlay detection boundary boxes) to a live streaming web page. We are stationed at this intersection and visit this web page via a mobile phone to monitor and inspect the detection results in real time. A snapshot of the detected live traffic condition is illustrated in Fig. 8, showing that most of the essential targets (i.e., cars, persons, bikes, and traffic signs) are recognized properly.

Fig. 8. Snapshot of detected traffic condition

In order to compare the performances between edge-based and cloud-based paradigms, we deploy the same application on a China Unicom's cloud host which is located in a data center about 1800 km away from the intersection. This cloud sever shares the same configurations as our MEC host, ensuring the same computing capabilities. By comparing the timestamps of a specific frame at the point of camera capture and renderer output, we can get the system delay and the corresponding jitter of our application. The calculated delay includes both transmission and computation latencies, where the former mainly depends on the transmission distance of the IP packages, while the latter depends on the computing capability. Moreover, in order to compare the actual status of network usage, we obtain the records of system throughput from the MEC and cloud platform managers respectively. We utilize a 100-s (containing 3000 frames) video clip to calculate the system performances of delay, jitter, and throughput. The average delay is the mean value of the above mentioned timestamp difference between 3000 frames, and the corresponding jitter is the mean value of the deviation from the calculated average delay. The average system throughput is calculated as the total transmitted data divided by total 100 s. The performances between edge-based and cloud-based systems are compared in Table 1.

Table 1. Performance comparison between edge-based and cloud-based systems

Infrastructure	Delay	Jitter	Throughput
Edge	37.25 ms	0.53 ms	643.36 Mbps
Cloud	183.62 ms	10.45 ms	437.19 Mbps

The above experimental results show that our proposed edge-based paradigm outperforms the conventional cloud-based scheme. Limited by the complexity of routing, the nearer the IP packages are transmitted, the better the system performs in latency and bandwidth. Our 5G MEC based application takes the advantages of both 5G network and edge computing, ensuring low latency, high stability, high bandwidth and powerful computing capability, and is more suitable for real-time scenarios compared to the cloud-based paradigm.

It is worth noting that the TCO (total cost of ownership) of edge-based application is higher than that of conventional cloud-based scheme, due to the much smaller scale of the edge computer clusters and the much more complex management of the distributed edge data centers. Therefore, the advantages of edge computing and cloud computing are complementary to each other by trading off performance and TCO, with the former being more suitable for critical applications and the latter more suitable for general cases.

4   Conclusion

The integrated 5G MEC system brings network, computing and devices together in a converged ecosystem, becoming the key enabler for intelligent transformation of vertical industries. This paper introduces the integrated 5G MEC system and proposes a 5G MEC based intelligent video application of panoramic object detection. An on-site experiment is performed to validate the feasibility and performance of the proposed application, and the experimental results show that our edge-based system outperforms the conventional cloud-based scheme in latency and bandwidth. By trading off performance and cost, the paradigm of 5G MEC can be utilized as a complementary of cloud computing for deploying critical applications. In the future, more and more IT system will choose the deployment mode of "Cloud-Edge Collaboration" to fulfill the challenging requirements of performance and cost in various vertical industry scenarios.

References

1. ITU-R M.2083: IMT Vision - "Framework and overall objectives of the future development of IMT for 2020 and beyond". ITU Recommendation (2015)
2. ETSI MEC. https://www.etsi.org/technologies/multi-access-edge-computing
3. Kekki, S., et al.: MEC in 5G networks. ETSI White Paper **28**, 1–28 (2018)
4. ETSI GR MEC 031 V2.1.1: Multi-access Edge Computing (MEC); MEC 5G Integration. ETSI Group Report (2020)
5. Liu, H., Chen, S., Kubota, N.: Intelligent video systems and analytics: a survey. IEEE Trans. Ind. Inf. **9**(3), 1222–1233 (2013). https://doi.org/10.1109/TII.2013.2255616
6. Shao, Z., Cai, J., Wang, Z.: Smart monitoring cameras driven intelligent processing to big surveillance video data. IEEE Trans. Big Data **4**(1), 105–116 (2018). https://doi.org/10.1109/TBDATA.2017.2715815
7. Hussain, T., Muhammad, K., Ser, J.D., Baik, S.W., de Albuquerque, V.H.C.: Intelligent embedded vision for summarization of multiview videos in IoT. IEEE Trans. Ind. Inf. **16**(4), 2592–2602 (2020). https://doi.org/10.1109/TII.2019.2937905
8. Hoang, V.T., Huang, D.S., Jo, K.H.: 3-D facial landmarks detection for intelligent video systems. IEEE Trans. Ind. Inf. **17**(1), 578–586 (2021). https://doi.org/10.1109/TII.2020.2966513
9. 3GPP TS 23.501 V16.8.0: Technical Specification Group Services and System Aspects; System architecture for the 5G System (5GS); Stage 2 (Release 16). 3GPP Technical Specification (2021)
10. ETSI GS MEC 003 V2.1.1: Multi-access Edge Computing (MEC); Framework and Reference Architecture. ETSI Group Specification (2019)
11. China Unicom. http://chinaunicom.com/news/202004/1588145294070068184.html
12. NVIDIA Developer. https://developer.nvidia.com/deepstream-sdk
13. GStreamer. https://gstreamer.freedesktop.org/

Research on Grid-Connected Model of Distributed Generation Based on Colored Petri Net

Bin Chen[1], Qiang Han[2(✉)], Huan Xu[1], Yuxiang Guo[2], Jie Li[2], and Tairan Song[2]

[1] Big Data Digitalization Department, China Southern Power Grid Co., Ltd.,
Guangzhou 510663, Guangdong, China
[2] Macau University of Science and Technology, Macau, China

Abstract. With the strategy of "Emission Peak" and "Carbon Neutrality" proposed the transformation and reform of the energy system are imminent. Building a new power system mainly composed of renewable power is one of the most important measures to achieve the dual goals on carbon. The stability and reliability of the new power system have become the focus of attention. Therefore, it is necessary to minimize the impact of distributed generation integration on the power system and find out the optimal configuration model. By studying the working mechanism of distributed generation such as wind power generation, photovoltaic power generation and energy storage power supply, this paper studies and summarizes the working strategy and operation mode during distributed power grid-connected and islanded operation, and further designs the distributed generation integration model based on Colored Petri Net for optimization. By deducing the configuration optimization of the grid connection model from the grid connection access point, network loss and economy, the analysis logic of the optimal grid connection access point, optimal grid connection capacity and optimal configuration is finally output. The method deduction shows that the grid connection model provides a new grid connection optimization method for distributed generation grid connection, which makes up for the relative instability of traditional grid connection in power system.

Keywords: New power system · Distributed generation · Grid-connected model · Colored Petri Net

1 Introduction

In September 2020, China made a solemn commitment at the 75th session of the United Nations General Assembly to "achieve peak carbon and carbon neutrality." In March 2021, China once again made an important deployment of "carbon peaking and carbon neutral," emphasizing the need to build a new power system with new energy as the mainstay, which clearly defines the direction of China's energy and power transformation development under the background of "double carbon." To achieve the national "carbon peak, carbon neutral" strategy, energy is the main battlefield, and electricity is the main

© Springer Nature Switzerland AG 2022
L.-J. Zhang (Ed.): EDGE 2021, LNCS 12990, pp. 50–62, 2022.
https://doi.org/10.1007/978-3-030-96504-4_4

force [1]. The construction of a new power system with new energy as the main body is one of the most important measures to achieve the goal of "double carbon." Among the new energy sources, photovoltaic power generation and wind power are the two types of power generation with the most mature technology and economy, the fastest development, and the largest scale effect in the world, and they are the expected main sources of new energy increments.

Unlike the traditional centralized large-scale power generation, new energy sources are mainly distributed power sources, which are close to the center of users, have relatively small generation capacity compared with large grid and are usually connected to power systems below 10 kV. For distribution grids, microgrid can relieve the pressure of supplying load to the large grid and supply power directly to the users. When the utility power fails to supply the load, it would turn into an islanded operation. The microgrid supply would continue to supply power, which would greatly enhance the reliability of the whole grid system. However, when the microgrid supply is connected to the utility to supply the load directly, it would change the relay protection mode of the whole system and affect the direction of the tide, which would certainly cause fluctuations to the power system and is not conducive to the planning management and scheduling operation of the whole power industry. With the fluctuating jumps and randomness of new energy generation, the microgrid supply would aggravate the uncertainty of the power system and reduce the power quality of the whole power network and the stability of the whole system to a greater extent [2].

With the introduction of the new power system, the grid connection of distributed power sources can enhance the environmental friendliness of power grid, reduce the net loss of power system, improve the utilization rate of renewable energy, and ensure the energy supply of the power system. Due to the instability and randomness of distributed power sources themselves, the whole power system is easily in an unstable state, especially the moment after the grid connection of distributed power sources [3]. Therefore, this paper proposes a method to construct a grid-connection model for distributed power sources based on colored Petri network, aiming to analyze the grid-connection model from three aspects of node voltage variation, power system network loss and economy, and to derive the optimal grid-connection access point, grid-connection capacity, and distribution network configuration.

2 Petri Net Model

The Petri Net has been applied by domestic and foreign researchers in grid fault diagnosis and distributed power supply energy coordination optimization because of their good parallel computing and matrix operation capabilities and convenient graphical representation, which can provide a good description of discrete and concurrent events. In the literature, a regionally integrated energy system model is proposed from the basic principles of energy consumption analysis, combined with the specific modeling principles of fuzzy Colored Petri Net with time constraints. In the paper, fault diagnosis method of the power system with improved temporal fuzzy Petri nets is proposed to fully use the temporal characteristics of power system faults [4].

The traditional Petri Net model is composed of place, transition, directed arc, and token elements. In a Petri Net model, the place is represented by a circle, the transition

52   B. Chen et al.

is represented by a rectangular box, the directed arc is used to connect the place and transition, and the token represents a dynamic object in the place that can be moved from one place to another, which is graphically represented as shown in Fig. 1. The Petri Net of finite capacity is a six-tuple denoted as (P, T, I, O, M, K). $P = \{p_1, p_2, \dots, p_m\}$ denotes the set of finite places. $T = \{t_1, t_2, \dots, t_n\}$ denotes the set of finite transitions, $P \cup T \neq \varnothing, P \cap T = \varnothing; I: P \times T \to \mathbf{N} = \{0, 1, 2, \dots\}$ is the input function. $O: P \times T \to \mathbf{N}$ is the output function. $M: P \to \mathbf{N}$ represents the identifier of the number of tokens in the place, and M_0 is the initial identifier. $K: P \to \{1, 2, \dots\}$ is the capacity function, and $K(p)$ denotes the maximum number of tokens that can be held in the place. $\bullet t = \{p: p \in P \text{ 且 } I(p, t) > 0\}$ denotes the set of predecessors of transition t, which represents the set of all input places pointing to t [5]. $t^\bullet = \{p: p \in P \text{ 且 } O(p, t) > 0\}$ denotes the posterior set of the transition t, which denotes the set of all places output from t. Similarly, the predecessor set of the p can be denoted as $\bullet p = \{t \in T: O(p, t) > 0\}$ and the posterior set of p can be denoted as $p^\bullet = \{t \in T: I(p, t) > 0\}[6]$.

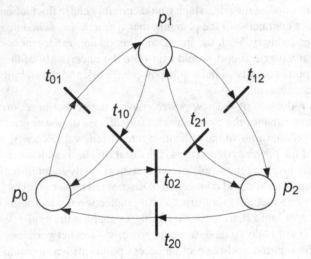

Fig. 1. Graphical instance of Petri Net

Colored Petri Net (CPN), as a type of advanced Petri Net, can simplify the model by using color as a special tool to represent resources of the same function or type. Its use of one model instead of multiple models with the same or approximate function, and this simplification enhances the generality of the model.

3   Working Mechanism of Distributed Power Supply

Since wind power and photovoltaic power generation are usually affected by the external environment, to better improve the stability of the output power of wind power generation, energy storage is usually added to microgrid to enhance the stability of the power system, so this paper intends to study the wind power storage microgrid [2].

3.1   Direct-Drive Wind Turbines for Power Generation

The direct-drive wind power system consists of a direct-drive wind turbine, a permanent magnet synchronous generator, a PWM rectifier with internal energy storage capacitors, a DC bus, a grid-side inverter, a high-pass filter circuit, and a large grid. In contrast to the double-fed wind turbine, the wind turbine no longer incorporates a gearbox and shares a common shaft with the synchronous generator. Hence, both have the same angular velocity, i.e., the same speed. The energy conversion process is the initial energy wind energy acts directly on the three blades of the direct-drive wind turbine. The energy at the wind turbine terminal is in the form of mechanical energy [7]. The generator input is mechanical energy, and after vectorial directional control, the final energy form is three-phase AC energy, which is first rectified to DC by the machine side rectifier and network side converter under the calibration of the control strategy, and finally inverted to AC by transformer step-up/down and then transmitted to the large grid.

According to the above power generation principle, when constructing the Petri Net model of a direct-drive wind power system, the core is to ensure its operation at the maximum point of power. To ensure the working condition of the wind turbine to maintain the maximum power for efficient operation, the optimal blade tip speed ratio method is used in the wind turbine system to adjust the rotational speed to find the optimal blade tip speed ratio by monitoring the characteristic parameter electromagnetic torque of the manipulated synchronous motor in real-time [8].

3.2   Photovoltaic Power Generation

When a single-stage grid-connected PV system is used, it is simpler than a wind turbine system, with only the inverter link in the grid-connected state, consisting of a combination of the PV array and the grid-connected inverter [9].

Photovoltaic cells are small, easy to combine and serve as the basic unit in a photo-voltaic module, combined in series-parallel to form the photovoltaic array required by the model to meet the actual load. It can be equated to a DC power supply consisting of a photogenerated current source and a diode connected in parallel, which is usually in the forward conduction state and does not switch back and forth between conduction and cutoff.

Combined with the volt-ampere characteristic curve of the PV array, to maximize the efficient use of solar energy, the maximum power tracking control is needed to change the PV array terminal voltage in real-time and maintain the maximum output power state.

3.3   Battery Energy Storage

When the battery storage system adopts the single-stage grid-connected system, the structure is like that of the photovoltaic system, with only the inverter link in the grid-connected state, which consists of a combination of the battery and the grid-connected inverter. The energy storage module has a dual function, which can help the microgrid maintain a more stable output state and provide a power system reference value for each micro-power when the utility power fails to ensure the reliability of the power system.

The battery storage system usually operates in parallel with other distributed power sources, i.e., the battery is directly connected to the grid through the network side converter. Due to the low rated voltage level of the battery itself, the "voltage limited charging and discharging" strategy is used to ensure that the charging process is closer to the optimal charging curve. This method needs to control the charging and discharging state of the battery through the network side converter, and the outer loop of the grid-connected inverter controls the DC side voltage of the battery, while the inner loop controls the DC, and the grid-connected voltage of the grid-connected inverter is adjusted to maintain the constant terminal voltage of the battery. This control method is "autonomous" and switches the charging and discharging states in conjunction with the load power demand [10].

4 Distributed Power Grid Connection Strategy and Model

4.1 Topology of Microgrid with Wind/Photovoltaic Power

The microgrid system architecture with scenic power supply studied in this paper consists of wind power generation system, photovoltaic array power generation system, battery storage system, primary load, and secondary load. The distributed power source is a solar photovoltaic array, and a direct-drive permanent magnet wind turbine, the energy storage system is a lithium-ion battery pack, where the energy conversion is mainly done by AC/DC three-phase PWM rectifier and DC/AC three-phase voltage grid-connected inverter. The dynamic load is used to simulate the power consumption load. The direct-drive permanent magnet wind turbine uses back-to-back dual PWM converters to regulate the output characteristics [11]. The PV array uses a single-stage PV grid-connected system, both of which are connected to the grid through a three-phase voltage grid-connected inverter to achieve the grid-connected effect. Renewable energy wind and solar power generation is limited by its volatility and instability, which cannot guarantee the power quality of the power system. Therefore, it is necessary to build an energy storage system to ensure the stable operation of the power system by switching the lithium-ion battery charging and discharging mode through control. The framework of the microgrid system with wind power, photovoltaic and battery is shown in Fig. 2.

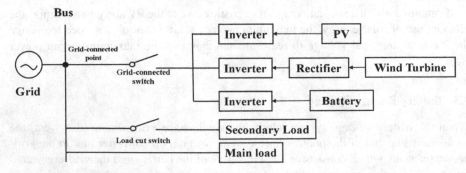

Fig. 2. Wind/Photovoltaic/Battery microgrid system architecture

4.2 Distributed Power Grid-Connected Strategy

In grid-connected operation, the microgrid is connected to the larger grid. In this operation mode, the active and reactive power output from the distributed power sources inside the microgrid is equal to its reference power, and the frequency and voltage adjustment is done by the larger grid. At the same time, there is an exchange of power between the external grid and the microgrid. The microgrid is supported by the large grid and operates in a stable state. If it is converted to islanded operation, the distributed power sources in the microgrid are allowed to generate electrical energy to supply the load without the support of the large grid, and this mode allows the microgrid to have a high-power supply security.

When grid-connected, the master-slave strategy is used to divide the micro-power sources into two categories, the main power source, and the slave power source. Based on the controllable characteristics of battery charging and discharging, the scenic storage microgrid studied in this paper uses the energy storage system as the main power source. All the main and slave power sources are controlled by constant power when running on the grid. The battery is controlled by constant voltage and constant frequency when operating in isolation, providing voltage and frequency reference signals to other microgrid sources in the off-grid state. Due to the limited energy storage capacity of the storage system, the minimum charge state needs to be set in order to protect the battery. Suppose the load demand in the microgrid system is higher than the power supply capacity of the storage system. In that case, the secondary load needs to be removed to ensure the continuous normal operation of the micro-grid system and reduce the power supply pressure.

4.3 Distributed Power Grid-Connected Mode

In grid-connected operation, the energy storage system is in a floating charge state, and the parameters of the power system are jointly determined by the grid and the microgrid. In islanded operation, the battery storage system acts as the main power source, providing reference voltage and frequency for the entire power system. The output power of the PV and wind power systems can supply the load and charge the energy storage system.

In this paper, the model of microgrid can detect the output power of battery storage system (P1), photovoltaic power generation system outputs power (P2), wind power generation system outputs power (P3) and load power (Pload). The different size relationship between the total output power of distributed power sources P_{total} and load power P_{load} would make the microgrid system in different working states.

In grid-connected mode, the energy storage system is in charging state:

1. Grid outputs the power: When $P_{total} > P_{load}$, the total energy emitted from the distributed power supply is greater than that required by the load, the energy storage system is in the charging state, and the microgrid would input the excess power to the grid, i.e., the grid absorbs the power from the microgrid;
2. Grid absorbs the power from microgrid: When $P_{total} < P_{load}$, the total energy from the distributed power supply is less than that required by the load, and the energy storage system is also in the charging state, but the grid supplies energy to the microgrid, and the grid supplies power to both the energy storage system and the load.

In islanded mode, with no support from the grid, the energy storage system performs autonomous conversion between charging and discharging according to the needs of the load:

1. Energy storage system is in charging state: When $P_2 + P_3 > P_{load}$, the total energy emitted from PV and wind power sources is greater than that required by the load, and in addition to supplying the load, the microgrid would input the excess power to the battery storage system, and the energy storage system is in charging state;
2. Energy storage system is in discharge state: When $P_2 + P_3 < P_{load}$, the total energy emitted by PV and wind power is less than that required by the load, the energy storage system is discharged, and all distributed power sources supply the load at the same time;
3. The secondary load is cut off: When $P_{total} < P_{load}$, the total energy emitted by PV power system, wind power system and energy storage system cannot meet the load demand, so the secondary load in the microgrid needs to be removed to ensure the normal operation of the microgrid in islanded operation.

5 Optimization Method of Grid-Connected Model Based on Colored Petri Net

5.1 Grid-Connected Model Based on CPN

The topological network of the power system is radial in shape. When constructing the grid-connected model, "power flow calculation" is used for analysis to plan the power capacity and find the optimal distributed power source. Take Fig. 3 as an example, the tide flows unidirectionally from the bus side to the load side, and there are two groups of loads in the figure, each representing a node. Starting from the source node, the voltage gradually decreases ($U_0 > U_1 > U_2$).

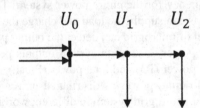

Fig. 3. Node voltage relationship in the distribution network

According to Fig. 3, the distributed power grid-connected model based on CPN is built as shown in Fig. 4.

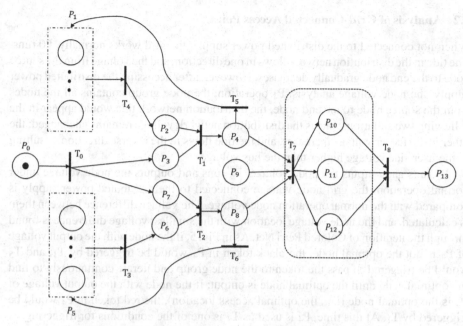

Fig. 4. Colored Petri Net model of distributed power supply

The physical meaning of the place is explained, as shown in Table 1.

Table 1. Physical significance of Petri Net Place

Place	Physical meaning
P_0	The grid operates normally and is not connected to a distributed generation
P_1	Distributed generation is connected to different voltage nodes
P_2	Output node voltage
P_3	Output node voltage under normal operation
P_4	Information feedback and output optimal node voltage position
P_5	Distributed generation is connected to the grid separately with different capacities
P_6	Output grid-connected capacity
P_7	Output the node load under normal operation
P_8	Information feedback and output of optimal grid-connected capacity
P_9	Control grid-connected inverters and regulate energy storage devices
P_{10}	Assess the cost of grid-connected line layouts and the impact of outages
P_{11}	Solve for the optimal configuration of energy storage devices
P_{12}	Solve for optimal reactive power compensation device configuration
P_{13}	Output grid-connected optimal configuration parameters

5.2   Analysis of Grid-Connected Access Point

When not connected to the distributed power supply, the grid works normally, P0 runs. The tide in the distribution network flows in one direction, and the voltage from the source node to the end node gradually decreases. However, after accessing the distributed power supply, the node voltage analysis, P_1 operation, the node group contains all the nodes from the source node to the end node, the distribution network tide would appear in the following two situations: one is the distribution network voltage remains unchanged; the other is the feeder voltage increases, and the tide flows in the reverse direction, resulting in the user side voltage higher than the bus voltage.

P_2 runs and outputs the node voltage, P_3 runs and outputs the node voltage under normal operation, the grid node voltage connected to the distributed power supply is compared with the normal operation node voltage. The voltage difference between them is calculated, and the node voltage location with the smallest voltage difference is found through the iteration of Colored Petri Net. As in Fig. 5, if the node with the output voltage of P_4 is not the optimal node, the black token in P_4 would be triggered by T_1, and T_5 would be triggered to pass the token to the node group and iterate continuously to find the optimal node until the optimal node is output; if the node with the output voltage of P_4 is the optimal node (i.e., the optimal access location), the red token in P_4 would be triggered by T_1. At this time, P_4 is used as T_7 is one of the conditions for triggering.

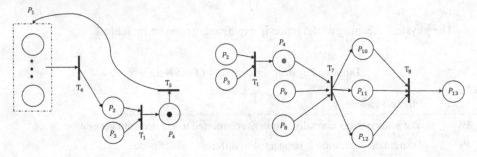

Fig. 5. Node triggering mechanism of Colored Petri Net

In the optimization process, it is necessary to avoid voltage crossing and power flow current reversal when the load is much smaller than the power output, so it is necessary to control the charging and discharging of grid-connected inverters and energy storage devices to prevent voltage crossing and reduce the voltage increase caused by the grid connection.

5.3   Analysis of Grid-Connected Capacity

Under normal conditions, the power system is in balance, P_0 operates, and the grid outputs power to supply the load. However, the access of distributed power sources leads to changes in the tide size and tide flow direction in the distribution network, and the network losses would increase with the power flow of the grid. To maintain the power balance of the distribution network, the optimal grid-connected capacity of distributed power sources needs to be found, and P_5 operates with the capacity group containing all the accessible grid-connected capacities. Considering the grid-connected capacity and system load, there are three cases of distributed power sources connected to the grid as follows:

Case 1: No change in the distribution network (undersupply): the total output power of all distributed power sources is less than the total load demand at the node, and the tide size and power flow direction do not change;

Case 2: Reverse tide (supply exceeds demand): the total output power of distributed power at the access node is greater than the total load demand of the node, but the total output power of distributed power of the system is less than the total load demand of the system, and the system generates reverse tide, and there is power reverse transmission;

Case 3: Power delivery to the upper grid (supply far exceeds demand): When the total output power of all distributed power sources in the system is greater than the total system load demand, there is a surplus of power, which would make power delivery to the upper grid.

P_6 would output the grid-connected capacity of the distributed power supply, and P_7 would output the node load under the grid not connected to the distributed power supply. According to the grid-connected capacity and the system load, we would judge which of the above cases belongs to the grid-connected capacity after connecting to the distributed power supply. The optimal grid-connected capacity would make the distribution grid not change when the distributed power supply is connected to the grid, which is in case one, and the distributed power supply can provide the load maximally, so we need to iterate continuously to find the optimal grid-connected capacity. As in Fig. 6, if the node of P_8 output power is not the optimal grid connection capacity, then after T_2 trigger, the black token in P_8 would trigger T_6, and the token would be passed to the capacity group and iterate continuously to find the optimal grid connection capacity until the optimal grid connection capacity is output; if the node of P_8 output power is the optimal grid connection capacity, then after T_2 trigger, the red token in P_8, and at this time, P_8 is used as one of the conditions for T_7 trigger. P_8 is used as one of the conditions of the T_7 trigger.

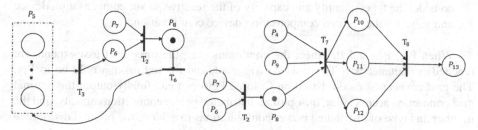

Fig. 6. Capacity triggering mechanism of Colored Petri Net

In the process of finding the optimal solution, it is necessary to ensure that after the distributed power supply is connected to the grid, the grid-connected capacity and the load are quickly balanced, P_9 operation, calculating the capacity balance point, mainly considering the grid-connected inverter control and energy storage device regulation, preventing the voltage from crossing the limit by controlling the voltage value and the charging and discharging of the energy storage device, and then realizing the power balance of the system.

When P_4, P_8 and P_9 get the token simultaneously, then T_7 would be triggered to output the optimal access point location and power capacity configuration of the distributed power supply to the grid. After the grid connection location and power capacity are determined, the model basis would be laid for the configuration of the number of PV, wind turbines and energy storage batteries, so it is necessary to consider further the economic cost of the whole power system from the economic point of view.

5.4 Analysis of Grid-Connected Cost

When the optimal grid access point and optimal grid capacity are determined, the number of turbines and individual capacity, the number and parameters of PV panels, and the configuration of energy storage devices need to be searched for, so a comprehensive economic assessment is made from the following three aspects, starting from the cost of the whole power system:

1. Cost of network layout: the access of distributed power supplies would make the network layout change, even causing some lines to be disconnected, after P_{10} operation, to assess the increased line layout costs due to the access of distributed power supplies;
2. Cost of power supply equipment: distributed power supply represented by batteries can maintain the transient balance of switching between grid-connected and islanded operation, but it is necessary to consider the type, number, and parameter configuration of power supply units, P_{11} operation, and the configuration of power supply units to find the best;
3. Cost of Control device: After accessing the distributed power supply, the power balance must be considered. Due to the instability of the power supply, the compensation device needs to be dynamically adjusted, so P_{12} operation is required to consider the type, quantity and capacity of the reactive power compensation device and solve for the optimal compensation device configuration.

When P_{10}, P_{11} and P_{12} meet the conditions (i.e., the three cost assessments are reached) simultaneously, T_8 would be triggered, and the red token would be in P_{13}. The grid connection model based on Colored Petri Net can finally output the optimal grid connection access point, the optimal distributed power connection capacity, and the number and type of distributed power configurations to achieve the optimal distributed power connection model.

6 Conclusion

In this paper, we propose a distributed power supply grid-connected model based on Colored Petri Net. This model is applicable to new power system and large-scale distributed energy access. By studying the working mechanism of distributed power resources, analyzing five operation modes of distributed power sources in grid- connected and islanded operation, and performing optimization based on the Colored Petri Net, the optimization of grid connection model configuration is deduced from three aspects: node voltage, network loss and economy. This method extrapolates the analysis of distributed power supply grid connection and provides a new digital optimization method for distributed power supply grid connection. It lays a good model foundation for solving the insufficient stability of traditional power supply grid connection in power system and carrying out experimental verification, which has strong practical value.

In the future, the model would be used as the basis for exploring the optimal solution to output the optimal grid access point, the optimal grid capacity, and the optimal configuration of distributed power supply type and quantity. It can provide important support for the Southern Power Grid to accelerate the construction of a new power system and help the Southern Power Grid to realize the "three business" transformation.

References

1. Zhang, Y., Dai, Y.: Analysis on the uncertainty factors of pumped storage power station construction investment under the Chinese characteristic power market environment. In: IOP Conference Series: Earth and Environmental Science (2021)
2. Jia, L., Qin, Y., Suo, J., Feng, J., Diao, L., An, M. (eds.): EITRT 2017. LNEE, vol. 482. Springer, Singapore (2018). https://doi.org/10.1007/978-981-10-7986-3
3. Wu, F., Xu, G., Qi, Z., Qi, Z., Zhang, M., He, R.: Research on multi-level distribution strategy based on energy internet. In: E3S Web of Conferences (2021)
4. Shen, X.J., Zhang, Y., Chen, Sh.: Investigation of grid-connected photovoltaic generation system applied for Urban Rail Transit energy-savings. In: 2012 IEEE Industry Applications Society Annual Meeting (2012)
5. Liu, Z., Wu, N., Yang, F.: Petri net-based scheduling of time constrained single-arm cluster tools with wafer revisiting. Adv. Mech. Eng. 8 (2016)
6. Yang, F., Wu, N., Qiao, Y., Zhou, M.: Optimal scheduling of single-arm multi-cluster tools with two-space buffering modules. In: 2014 IEEE International Conference on Automation Science and Engineering (CASE) (2014)
7. Ai, C., Zhou, G., Wang, Y., Gao, W., Kong, X.: Active power control of hydraulic wind turbines during low voltage ride-through (LVRT) based on hierarchical control. Energies 12, 1224 (2019)
8. Chen, S., Ma, Y., Ma, L., Qiao, F., Yang, H.: Early warning of abnormal state of wind turbine based on principal component analysis and RBF neural network. In: 2021 6th Asia Conference on Power and Electrical Engineering (ACPEE) (2021)
9. Bai, D., Cao, H., Wang, L.: Research and simulation of V2G technology in micro grid. In: 2016 China International Conference on Electricity Distribution (CICED) (2016)

10. Tong, X., Yan, C., Wang, J., Yang, S., Tang, K., Li, C.: DC voltage follow-up control for mitigating the power fluctuation of distributed generation. In: IECON 2017 - 43rd Annual Conference of the IEEE Industrial Electronics Society (2017)
11. Dong, X., Li, X., Cheng, S.: Energy management optimization of microgrid cluster based on multi-agent-system and hierarchical Stackelberg game theory. IEEE Access **8**, 206183–206197 (2020)

Study on the Sustainable Development of Community Home-Based Elderly Care

Wei Wei[✉] and Feng Luyao

Shenzhen Institute of Information Technology, Shenzhen 518172, SZ, China
{2018000208,fengly}@sziit.edu.cn

Abstract. The population in China gradually shows the characteristics of "aging" and "less children" making the traditional model of "raising children for elderly care" difficult to sustain. Since 2013, each district and street in Shenzhen, Guangdong province has established an elderly care center. After four or five years of exploration, three types of elderly care models have been formed: "government building and running", "government building and private running" and "public assistance and government sponsorship." This research studied the development model of "public assistance and government sponsorship" of Shenzhen Siben Elderly Company, and found that it also faced similar problems to other pilot cities in china, such as poor cooperation with the government, a lack of funds, and insufficient management. Leveraging the unique advantages in the fields of Internet, finance, real estate, etc. of Shenzhen City, the company has evolved a new sustainable development model for elderly care. Our study proposes corresponding policy suggestions based on the problems and advantages of this model, so as to provide ideas and reference for the improvement of community home-based elderly care in China.

Keywords: Shenzhen · Internet · Finance · Community home-based elderly care · Sustainable development

1 Introduction

Affected by the one-child policy and the growing number of elderly people, China is facing huge challenges in solving problems to do with the elderly, and is also facing a crisis of "getting old before getting rich" [1, 2]. By the end of 2018, there were 249.49 million people aged 60 years and older, which indicates an increase of .59 million over the previous year, and accounts for 17.9% of the total population of China. The Academy of Social Sciences released the "Blue book of the great health industry: development report of the great health industry in China", which predicted that by 2050, the number of elderly people aged 60 and above in China will reach 483 million, and that those aged 80 and above will reach 108 million. Figure 1 shows a forecast of the number of elderly people over the age of 60 in China between 2020 and 2050.[1]

---

[1] Please refer to http://www.gov.cn/zhengce/2019-11/21/content_5454347.htm.

© Springer Nature Switzerland AG 2022
L.-J. Zhang (Ed.): EDGE 2021, LNCS 12990, pp. 63–74, 2022.
https://doi.org/10.1007/978-3-030-96504-4_5

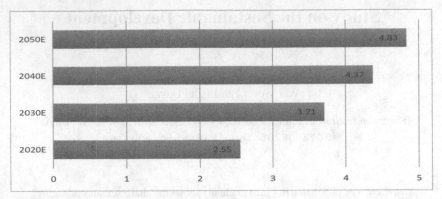

Fig. 1. Forecasts for the number of elderly people over the age of 60 in China from 2020 to 2050.

Against this background, in November 2019, the State Council of China issued the "National medium and long-term planning for actively addressing population aging (see Footnote 1)." Covering the near future to 2022, the medium term to 2035, and the long-term outlook to 2050, this plan is a strategic, comprehensive, and guiding document for China to actively respond to population aging by the middle of this century. The plan considers whether easing population aging could be a necessary guarantee for achieving high-quality economic development. Specifically, this plan deploys specific tasks to cope with five aspects of population aging: strengthening the social wealth reserve; improving the effective labor supply; building a high-quality system of services and products for the elderly; promoting technological innovation; and constructing a good social environment for rearing, filial piety, and respecting the elderly.

Exploring a sustainable development model for elderly care in China is the focus of this research. After selecting Shenzhen Siben Aging Enterprise Development Co., Ltd. as the research object, we conducted visits and in-depth interviews to understand the status and existing problems of community home-based elderly care in Shenzhen City. This research aimed to provide a policy basis for a timely and scientific response to population aging in Shenzhen City, and also to provide a reference for improving the operation and practice of the community home-based care model in Shenzhen City and the development of China's home-based elderly care system. This research makes three main contributions: first, the primary data obtained through field research from Shenzhen Siben Elderly Company show the current status of elderly care companies in Shenzhen city, thus enriching existing literature in the pension field; second, it summarizes the current "public assistance and government sponsorship" model implemented and explored by the elderly care institutions of Shenzhen City, as it has certain referential significance for other cities in China; third, it discusses models such as "Internet + elderly care", "finance + elderly care," "real estate + elderly care," and other elderly care models, and then proposes innovative and responsive suggestions.

2 Literature Review

In recent years, the market-oriented development of elderly care has become the focus of scholarly attention. Chinese scholar Suo Lingyan [3] pointed out that during the transition period, China's elderly care security system should define the relationship between the government and the market, continue to deepen reform of the elderly care insurance system, and reduce pressure on the government while maintaining a market-oriented approach. Tong Chunfen et al. [4] believed that only by injecting market elements into the elderly care security system can elderly care policy progress from an emergency strategy to simultaneous coordination with sustainable economic and social development. Through model construction Yan Chengliang [5] found that compared with the social care provided by the government, care provided by the market would correspond to a higher birth rate and greater social welfare.

By comparing the background of socio-economic development and the living conditions of the elderly, living styles, income differences, and the cost of elderly care under different models, Chinese scholars have concluded that community home-based elderly care is more economical than home-based elderly care and institutional elderly care. Zhang Ge [6] pointed out that community home-based elderly care was based on the family and society, and was a diverse care system in which the family, community, state, non-profit organizations, and the market participated together. Its service providers were mainly community-based social service systems, which had the characteristics of diversified service subjects, publicized service targets, diversified service methods, and professionalized service teams. Wei Pu [7] analyzed the different elderly care models and living styles of urban and rural old people by collecting data from an urban and rural elderly sample survey in 2003. He believed that although there was a large difference in the elderly security system between the urban and rural areas, the elderly in both urban and rural areas tended to choose home-based elderly care in terms of the way they lived. Sun Zhong [8] believed that home-based elderly care could save social costs and make full use of resources compared with institutional elderly care. The coverage of home-based elderly care was wide and community-based elderly care services were comprehensive and targeted.

However, the sustainable development of home-based elderly care in China still faces severe challenges. Zhang Xiaoting [9] argued that in the community, the government purchased parts of home-based elderly care. Owing to the limited human, financial, and material resources of the government and community, the provision of welfare home-based elderly care was insufficient. In 2019, the Research Group of the Ministry of Social Affairs, Development Research Center of the State Council pointed out that, as a whole, China's elderly care system relied heavily on elderly care institutions, attached too much importance to hardware construction, and lacked development of home-based and community-based elderly care; affected by the trend in consumption and the ability to pay, the elderly were generally unwilling or unable to pay for elderly care services, which effectively led to insufficient demand, restricted the development of the elderly care industry, and, in turn, affected the fulfillment of elderly care needs [10].

It is not difficult to find that the emergence and development of the home-based elderly care model in China has undergone a long and complicated exploratory process, and that the marketization of elderly care needs to be expanded. From a detailed perspective on the problem, home-based elderly care is not only a social security issue that affects peoples' livelihood but also a major issue related to the development of the elderly care industry and the long-term sustainable development of the economy (Table 1).

Table 1. Summary of prior findings on the development of home-based elderly care.

Content	Authors	Main conclusion
Marketization of elderly care has become the focus of scholarly attention	Suo Lingyan [3] Tong Chunfen et al. [4] Yan Chengliang [5]	During the transition period, China's elderly care security system should define the relationship between the government and the Tong market, continue to deepen reform of the elderly care insurance system, and reduce pressure on the government while maintaining a market-oriented approach. Compared with the social care provided by the government, that provided by the market would correspond to a higher birth rate and social welfare
Home-based elderly care has become an inevitable choice for Chinese elderly in the new situation	Zhang Ge [6] Wei Pu [7] Sun Zhong [8]	Home-based elderly care has the characteristics of diversified service subjects, publicized service targets, diversified service methods, and professionalized service teams. China's population aging is characterized by getting old before getting rich, and home-based elderly care has the advantages of low cost, wide coverage, and flexible service methods
The sustainable development of home-based elderly care in China still faces severe challenges	Zhang Xiaoting [9] Research Group of the Ministry of Social Affairs, Development Research Center of the State Council in China [10]	Home-based elderly care faces insufficient supply, low levels of specialization, a lack of service supervision system, etc. The elderly care system as a whole relies heavily on elderly care institutions, resulting in insufficient effective demand and restricting the development of the elderly care industry

3 Methods and Materials

3.1 Background of Elderly Care in Shenzhen City

Since 2013, each district and street in Shenzhen City has established an elderly care center. After four or five years of exploration, Shenzhen formed three types of elderly care models: government built and run, government built and privately run, and public assistance and government sponsorship. Among them, the model of "government built and run" is financed and operated by the government, but this model is only aimed at a small number of special groups, which plays a role in the bottom line. The government built and privately run model is financed by the government and operated by private enterprises. This model has been tried in Futian District, Shenzhen City; it requires that each elderly person stay in an elderly care institution for no more than six months. However, in practice, because not many elderly people stay in short-term care, the income generated cannot cover the cost, which becomes a point of contention. Third model, public assistance and government sponsorship, is advocated by the government for development; this is where the government provides properties while private enterprises are responsible for financing and operations. In this model, the government-provided property is the site; only some provide water and electricity. This model was launched in 2014, and corresponds to a market-based operation model. Currently, there are pilots in the districts of Longgang, Bao'an, Longhua, Yantian, and Nanshan in Shenzhen City. Bao'an District took the lead in proposing the construction of 100 elderly care institutions based on this model, and proposed a three-year construction plan for 2018–2020. According to the layout of Bao'an, Longgang District proposed building 111 such elderly care institutions within three years (2018–2020), and planned to achieve full coverage of 111 community projects in its district by the end of 2020. On the demand side, Ni Chidan and Li Liangjin [11] concluded that the growth rate of the elderly population in Shenzhen City exceeded the growth rate of the permanent population by 8.4 times, according to data from the Shenzhen Bureau of Statistics. In addition, according to China Mobile's big data estimating the 2018 population, Shenzhen's total population each day was stable above 25 million before the 2018 Spring Festival. It is apparent that the elderly population is growing fast and the population base is large. In 2016, there were 36 home-based non-governmental non-profit institutions for the elderly in Shenzhen City, which served 215,036 person-times throughout the year, and issued 24.642 million yuan in consumer service certificates for elderly care, with a utilization rate of 98% [12]. With the development of the elderly care industry, a large number of private enterprises have also actively invested in elderly care.

Until November 2019, through searching for the keywords "elderly care services", "aged services," and "Shenzhen" in "Qichacha," we collected data on 5,017 related companies. The majority, 3,256, were less than three years old; of the rest, 1,148 companies were 3–5 years old, 445 companies were 5–10 years old, and only 168 were older than 10 years. This shows that in the past three years, the number of companies has increased by thousands, indicating that investment in the elderly care industry has rapidly progressed. However, the statuses shown by these companies are mostly continuous, and only a small proportion are in business. There are even many companies that have been written off and revoked, mostly over the last five years. This suggests that Shenzhen has a relatively broad market for elderly care development, but companies' operational development still faces many problems: services are mostly provided by non-profit organizations, market players participate insufficiently, services lack competition, service content is single and quality is low, the overall marketization degree of home-based care is not high, and Shenzhen's advantages and characteristics have not been fully reflected upon and brought into play. Of course, after more than ten years of accumulating practical experience as a leading area of demonstration for building socialism with Chinese characteristics, the core city of the Greater Bay Area of Guangdong-Hong Kong-Macao has the highest degree of marketization in China. Shenzhen has also discovered its own unique standards on elderly care. By studying its experience, we aim to both gradually promote the development process of home-based care in Shenzhen and explore an innovative path for addressing the development difficulties of home-based elderly care in China (Table 2).

Table 2. Comparison of three elderly care models

Elderly care model	Coordination form	Service object	Problems
Government built and run	Government investment plus government operation	Three "nos" elderly	Fewer people covered
Government built and privately run	Government provides the site, equipment and decoration, and the private enterprise operates services	Community elderly	Short-term non-permanent, "respite" service; not many elderly people are staying as they cannot cover the cost
Public assistance and government sponsorship	Government provides only the venue; private enterprises are responsible for equipment, decoration, and operations	Community elderly	There are pinch points in the "run-in" cooperation between enterprises and the government

Note: "Three nos" means no working ability, no source of livelihood, and no dependents.

3.2 Methods

To understand the development status of home-based elderly care enterprises in Shenzhen in depth, this study selected Shenzhen Siben Elderly Care Company as a typical case for illustration. Shenzhen Siben Elderly Company Development Co., Ltd. was established in July 2014 with registered capital of 10 million yuan. Since 2007, the company's ounder has begun to explore the "public assistance and government sponsorship" model of elderly care in practice.[2] The company was rated in the "Top Ten Enterprises Respecting the Elderly" by Guangdong Province. It participated in promoting the policy formulation

[2] The development road of Siben elderly care industry—Tencent Video, v.qq.com.

for elderly care and the reform plans the of governments of China, Shenzhen, and multiple regions. Through practicing factual analysis, the company promoted the integration of community home-based elderly care into the national strategy. At present, the company has tried four sites in Shenzhen. Among them, the Yinhu community in Luohu District and the Zhangshubu community in Longgang District have been more successful than the others. About 3 million yuan is invested into each site. There are almost eight service personnel in each center, serving about 50 elderly people each day. The total number of registered elderly people in each center is about 1,000 persons, who are managed by big data systems. The elderly care model in Siben Company is typical of the development of home-based elderly care in Shenzhen. Researching it can master its accumulated experience and identify the problems of home-based elderly care in Shenzhen at a certain level. Using a question list (see Appendix 1 for details), we conducted and recorded semi-structured face-to-face interviews with the founder and several managers of Siben Company, each lasting for 60–90 min. All interviewees were informed of the research intent. The researchers also visited the elderly care center of Siben Company to undertake field observations. Figure 2 shows the daily business activities of the Siben elderly care center.

Fig. 2. The daily business activities of Siben Elderly Care Company

4   Results

The founders and managers of Shenzhen Siben Elderly Care Company reported similar problems with the overall development of community home-based elderly care as those encountered in other cities and regions. However, the company also has its own development potentiality and characteristics. Figure 3 shows the "public assistance and government sponsorship" model of Siben Company.

The survey results lead to the following conclusions:

1) In terms of funding, the "public assistance and government sponsorship" model of Siben Company has not yet become stable and consistently profitable. The source of

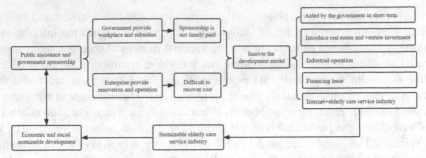

Fig. 3. The "public assistance and government sponsorship" model of Siben Company

funding is mainly divided into two parts: government funding and self-revenue. Of these, government funding forms the main proportion, covering the cost of Siben's elderly care centers. The government determines funding quotas based on site area, the number of elderly people served, and actual expenditure on the daily maintenance of facilities and equipment. The details are shown in Table 3; because each of the company's elderly care centers has an area of about 300 m², it can receive a corresponding 400,000 yuan of project area subsidy each year. In addition to the subsidies for service objects and maintenance costs, the annual subsidy from Siben Company is 40–50 thousand yuan. At the same time, the company can obtain self-revenue by carrying out physical rehabilitation therapy, technology assistance, and other services for the elderly. However, owing to the government's funding approval and complex procedures, etc., the funds are not dispersed in a timely manner and Siben often requires advance funding. In addition, the company is currently not receiving third-party gifts or donations.

Table 3. The government subsidy standards for community home-based elderly care

Subsidized projects	Subsidy funding standards
Site area	If the construction area is less than 300 m², the annual subsidy is 300,000 yuan; If the construction area is 300–500 m², the annual subsidy is 400,000 yuan; If the construction area is more than 500 m², the annual subsidy is 600,000 yuan
Number of elderly people served	The service object is subsidized by 150 yuan per person per month, and the elderly must person be served for more than 15 days per month
Costs of facilities and equipment maintenance	Subsidy according to actual expenditure

Note: The subsidy standards come from Office Document [2018] No. 182 of the Leading Group, "The Large Bowl Vegetables of the People's Livelihood, Longgang District, Shenzhen"

2) In terms of service objects, the "public assistance and government sponsorship" model of Siben Company mainly serves healthy and semi-disabled people. The semi-disabled population is relative to the disabled population. The "disabled elderly" refers to the elderly who have completely lost the ability to take care of themselves. The grading of self-care ability is defined in accordance with internationally accepted standards, including six criteria for eating, dressing, getting in and out of bed, going to the toilet, walking indoors, and taking a bath. Because the cost of care for disabled people is too high, Siben's elderly care centers, like other similar institutions, find it difficult to bear the medical services and labor costs of caring for this group, so it is currently unable to cover their care.

3) In terms of service content, the company mainly provides daytime comprehensive services such as living care, a supply of meals, health rehabilitation, psychological counseling, and recreational activities for the elderly in the community. The company pays attention to the service guarantee and emotional needs of the elderly, and provides convenient, fast, high-quality, and humanized services for them.

4) In terms of service methods, the company has "marketization + Internet" thinking, realized in an online and offline linkage services platform. The online service forms a system, including online appointments, online consultations, and online inquiry through the Internet, which greatly increases the probability of service conversion. The offline service forms an efficient operation model by optimizing service quality and expanding market influence. The company usually uses smart devices to collect data on the heart rate, blood pressure, chronic diseases, and other physical signs of the elderly, together with their needs information; it then sends these data and information to the online platform. The company introduced Japan's KCIS intelligent nursing system, with 8 million person-times nursing big data, as the basis for building a professional, comprehensive, and reliable health management and nursing service platform for the elderly.

5) In terms of the appointment of management and service personnel, the company can also meet the care needs of the elderly in the elderly care center. In terms of age level, the company's employees are not all elderly service personnel, and there are a large number of young caregivers who have been educated and trained, such as college students who have just graduated from the medical and nursing profession. In terms of staff stability, the company mainly retains service staff by improving salary satisfaction and recognition of the elderly care center.

6) In terms of the profit model, the company has high costs and low returns, so it is necessary to further explore market-oriented reform. In the "public assistance and government sponsorship" model, the government provides only venues, while the private enterprise is responsible for investment and operations. As investment in the elderly care industry requires sizable assets, including site decoration, purchase, and maintenance of the elderly care equipment, cost recovery is difficult. When investment conditions and value are unavailable, it is difficult for the company to recover costs. However, as a benchmarking enterprise for elderly care in Shenzhen and Guangdong Province, Siben Company relies on Shenzhen, an important global financial center, to introduce capital through direct management, shareholding, and opening guidance, aimed at eventually realizing the national brand chain operation.

7) In terms of cooperation with the government, it is difficult for the two sides to achieve coordination. The "public assistance and government sponsorship" model of elderly care cannot be separated from the cooperation of investors and government support. However, the company faces two significant pinch points in its cooperation with the government. First, elderly care programs are generally unpopular in the market. Elderly care investment is asset-heavy, and venture capital and angel investors are afraid to enter the elderly care industry. More importantly, investors generally believe that cooperation with the government is too risky, because government decisions often change considerably, so they dare not distribute venues too quickly or too often. Second, the government's actions are not market behaviors. The economic benefits pursued by enterprises are often contrary to the social benefits advocated by the government. The large number of constraints often limit companies' motivation to get involved.

5 Enlightenment for Sustainable Development of Home-Based Elderly Care in China

5.1 To Further Improve Government Planning of the Elderly Care Industry and Clarify the government's Duties and Powers

The government needs to consciously select powerful and caring companies to cooperate with and thereby cultivate them into elderly care enterprises of a certain size. At the same time, the government should handle the relationship between the welfare and profitability of elderly undertakings, provide enterprises with support in terms of land, taxation, and policies, and guide and cultivate social forces to actively participate, so as to reduce these institutions' dependence on government subsidies and reduce the government's administrative interventions; by actually performing the duties of support, cultivation, guidance, and supervision, they can aim at achieving a healthy, orderly, and sustainable home-based elderly care model.

5.2 To Develop "Internet Plus Home-Based Elderly Care" and Build a Community Home-Based Elderly Care Chain and Service Platform

Market demand (information source and demand source) can be quickly obtained through the Internet, and various situations can be classified in the context of big data, which could reduce the operating costs. At the same time, the demanders can also choose the service companies they trust based on this platform. "Internet plus home-based elderly care" includes not only smart care service platforms, such as appointment management systems, evaluation systems, day care management systems, and standardized systems for integrated medical care, but also related industries for smart devices for the elderly. For example, there are more than 10,000 aging-related products on the market today. Common technology includes chronic disease monitoring products, intelligent assistive products such as crutches, smart watches, and entertainment products. In the future, the expansion and large-scale operation of elderly institutions will be inseparable from the application of Internet technology in management and personnel services. However, setting up such an investment platform requires considerable funding. It is not enough to rely on an elderly care company such as Siben. It also needs to be promoted with a professional service platform to create a comprehensive service-sharing platform.

5.3 To Promote Close Integration of the Elderly Care Industry with Insurance, Estate, and Financing

Regarding the role of family assets in home-based elderly care, many foreign countries use real estate mortgages for the payment of long-term elderly care costs, that is, elderly care through houses. In China's current real estate market, the rate of home ownership has been increasing, and the real estate transaction market is active; to a certain extent, a reverse mortgage on housing is feasible. According to a recent survey, the proportion of people willing and able to obtain elderly care from housing in Shanghai was 48.24% [13]. In the field of investment, the current development of the elderly's real estate in China is also supported by national policies, so many real estate developers are eager to try this option, and social funds have begun to accumulate in the elderly-related real estate industry. According to the insurance industry's estimations, the expected annual return on investment of insurance funds for community elderly care is about 10%, which compares favorably with the return rate of 3–4% for insurance funds' other investment targets, and the return period is about 10 years [14]. It is precisely because this kind of investment has relatively stable returns that many insurance funds have already entered the elderly real estatemarket, including Xinhua Life, China Life, and Taikang Life [15]. On the whole, however, the actual results are not good. It is still necessary to strengthen cooperation between the government, real estate industry, and financial institutions in designing and implementing these financial products.

5.4 To Expand the Scope of Integration in the Elderly Care Industry and Innovate Infinancing Lease Models

In terms of industrial integration, the elderly care industry is linked to not only finance and real estate but also all aspects of the consumer sector, such as various retail products (food, materials, clothing, elderly supplies, etc.). The equipment investment includes tens of thousands of products such as nursing beds, diapers, monitors, wheelchairs, crutches, and rehabilitation tools. In view of the risks in using elderly care products, financial leasing can be proposed to reduce the risk costs of purchasing for the elderly. At the same time, the company can obtain revenue through leasing and on-site disinfection. Only by increasing scale and industrialization can the costs actually be reduced. From the perspective of the national economy, the integration of the elderly care industry can eliminate the risks of the population aging crisis, promote economic structural transformation, and drive long-term economic growth.

Appendix 1

Interview questions list.

1. What are the main target groups of the Siben Elderly Care Company?
2. What are the service contents of the Siben Elderly Care Company?
3. What are the funding sources of the Siben Elderly Care Center?
4. How are managers and service personnel appointed?
5. What are the requirements for living in a Siben elderly care center?
6. What is the operating model of the Siben Elderly Care Company?
7. What is the role of the government in home-based elderly care?
8. What is the situation with social forces and individuals' participation in the Siben Elderly Care Company?
9. What challenges are faced in the process of providing home-based elderly care services? How are these solved?

References

1. Zhong, S., Zhao, Y., Ren, J.: Research on the phenomenon of "getting old before getting rich" among regions in China. Popul. Res. **1**, 63–73 (2015)
2. Yan, G.: Is China still "getting old before getting rich"?—based on the judgment of the "old"-"rich" relationship model. Soc. Policy Res. **1**, 11–24 (2019)
3. Lingyan, S.: The relationship between the government and the market in the formation of China's elderly care security system in the transition period. Econ. Sci. **1**, 60–73 (2013)
4. Chunfen, T.: The four-dimensional supply subject and responsibility position of China's elderly care security system: an analytical framework based on the paradigm of welfare pluralism. J. Xiangtan Univ. (Philosop. Soc. Sci.) **3**, 28–32 (2015)
5. Chengliang, Y.: Elderly care, birth rate and social welfare. Econ. Res. **4**, 122–135 (2018)
6. Zhang, G.: Research on the Fund Guarantee of Urban Home-Based Elderly Care Services, pp. 51–61. China Social Science Press (2016)
7. Wei, P.: Urban-rural disparity in the income sources of the elderly in China and the choice of elderly care mode. J. Chongqing Inst. Technol. **12**, 26–29 (2006)
8. Sun, Z.: Research on the model of urban community home-based elderly care. model in China under the background of population aging. Master's thesis (2011)
9. Zhang, X.: The structural dilemma and solution of home-based elderly care Zhejiang Soc. Sci.
10. Research Group of the Ministry of Social Affairs, Development Research Center of the State Council, International Experience and Chinese Practice in the Development of Elderly Care System, pp. 1–40. China Development Press (2019)
11. Ni, C., Li, L.: Research report on the development of China's elderly care service status and development strategies of the elderly care service industry in Shenzhen city, pp. 1–38. Huazhong University of Science and Technology Press (2018)
12. Ding, J.: Research report on the development of China's elderly care services, pp. 197–199 (2019)
13. Yan, C., Zhu, L., Zhang, X., Zhang, W.: Research on the elderly willingness of getting elderly care by houses in Shanghai city. Val. Eng. **8**, 318–319 (2011)
14. Zhang, G.: Research on the Fund Guarantee of Urban Home-Based Elderly Care Services, pp. 3–174. China Social Science Press (2016)
15. Zhang, Y.: Taikang Life Insurance's Nadi Construction District in Shanghai city, to build a "migratory bird-type" elderly community, 7th edn. International Financial News (2013)

Steps for Enterprise Data Compliance in China

Bingbing Yu[✉]

Financial Industry, Beijing, China
margie2002@sina.com

Abstract. Data is becoming more and more important in national security, public interest, national economy, people's livelihood and personal privacy. China has also continuously strengthened the supervision of data from legislation to law enforcement. Data compliance becomes very important to enterprises in China.

Keywords: Data compliance · Laws and regulations

1 Data Law in the Digital Age

In the era of digital economy, data has become one of the 5 key production factors together with land, labor, capital and technology. Data is an important production factor and a national basic strategic resource, which has become a global consensus. The identity and value of data have changed.

Data is becoming more and more important in national security, public interest, national economy, people's livelihood and personal privacy. China has also continuously strengthened data regulation from legislation to law enforcement.

'Cyber Security Law' [1] was issued in 2016 and officially implemented in June 2017. 'Cyber Security Law' provides a framework for 'Classified Protection of Cybersecurity System', 'Critical Information Infrastructure (CII)', 'User Information Protection System', and 'Monitoring, Early Warning and Emergency Disposal'. 'Cyber Security Law' is a law formulated to ensure cyber security, safeguard cyberspace sovereignty, national security and social public interests, protect the legitimate rights and interests of citizens, legal persons and other organizations, and promote the healthy development of economic and social informatization. It opened the first year of data compliance in China. Since then, the process of domestic data legislation has been fully started.

'Data Security Law' [2] was approved on June 10, 2021 and came into force on September 1, 2021. The law includes data classification and hierarchical protection, important data protection catalogue, data security risk early warning mechanism, data security emergency disposal mechanism, national security review mechanism of data activities, etc. It is an important guideline for the compliance of data processing activities. Relevant enterprises and individuals shall establish and improve the data security management system according to the law and take corresponding technical measures to ensure data security. In this law, punishment for violation of laws was strengthened.

'Personal Information Protection Law' [3] was approved on August 20, 2021 and came into force on November 1, 2021. The law puts forward higher requirements for

L.-J. Zhang (Ed.): EDGE 2021, LNCS 12990, pp. 75–84, 2022.
https://doi.org/10.1007/978-3-030-96504-4_6

personal information protection. Enterprises should undertake corresponding obligations as personal information processors and take management measures and technical means to ensure that personal information processing activities comply with the provisions of laws and administrative regulations. And enterprises should also prevent unauthorized access and disclosure, tampering and loss of personal information.

These three laws have become the "troika" of cyberspace governance and data protection. 'Cyber Security Law' is responsible for the overall governance of Cyberspace Security. 'Data Security Law' is responsible for the security, development and utilization of data processing activities. And 'Personal Information Protection Law' is responsible for the protection of personal information.

"Data" and "compliance" have attracted the attention of the public again and again. Data compliance has never been as important and urgent as today.

Data compliance will become a concept generally accepted by enterprises, and the concept of data compliance will be further improved, from single compliance to data asset management. As an enterprise, it should pay attention to the impact of relevant data regulations on enterprise compliance, so as to effectively avoid risks. Once there are loopholes in the management system, it may fall into a criminal trap.

The 3 important laws have been implemented, and a data legal regulation system that meets the needs of the times and China's national conditions has been established. This is an exciting legislative event, but also puts forward great challenges and tests for theory and practice. Enterprises need to reduce risks and achieve data compliance. Then how enterprise lands data compliance is a problem that everyone cares about and hopes to solve. In order to comply with regulations, A Data and Cyber Security Improvement Program is a good way for landing data compliance. Such program normally includes below 3 steps.

1. Gap analysis
2. Action plan
3. Implementation (Chart 1)

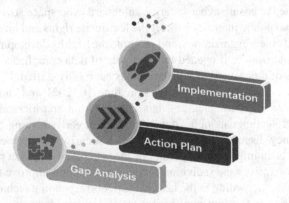

Chart 1. 3 steps for enterprise data compliance

2 Data and Cyber Security Improvement Program

2.1 Step One: Gap Analysis

An enterprise's good data compliance system is nothing more than an effective combination of technical measures and management measures. To do gap analysis also need consider these two aspects.

Gap analysis is one of the strategic analysis methods. Compare the requirements of laws and regulations with the current practice of enterprises, and analyze whether there is a gap between them. If there is a gap, further analyze the causes of the gap and formulate measures to reduce or eliminate the gap. Gap analysis is risk-based approach. The analysis is to identify data compliance risks.

The first step in gap analysis is to consider legal requirements. 'Cyber Security Law', 'Data Security Law' and 'Personal Information Protection Law' are the framework legislations. In order to effectively analyze the gap and better compare the current practice of the enterprise, it is necessary to refer to relevant national standards, industry standards and guidelines.

Such standards and guidelines play an obvious guiding and referential role in enterprise data compliance and law enforcement management. They indicate the direction for data compliance. Although they are not mandatory, not the only way for enterprises to implement data compliance, and the regulatory authorities cannot take them as a direct legal basis for administrative law enforcement, they provide good legal practice example for enterprises to implement data protection. Here are some examples of National standards and industry standards (in financial industry).

GB/T35273-2020 Information Security Technology – Personal Information Security Specification.

GB/T39335-2020 Information Security Technology – Guidance for Personal Information Security Impact Assessment.

GB/T37964-2019 Information Security Technology – Guidance for Personal Information De-identification.

JR/T0171-2020 Personal Financial Information Protection Technical Specification.

JR/T0197-2020 Financial data security—Guidelines for data security classification.

JR/T 0223-2021 Financial data security—Security specification of data life cycle.

JR/T0071-2012 Implementation guide for classified protection of information system of financial industry.

After understanding laws and regulations, relevant standards, specifications and guidance, enterprises can start gap analysis. Starting from technical and management measures, enterprises can deeply analyze the current practice of enterprises from five aspects: cross border data transfer, data management life cycle, management system, technical means and personal data subject rights.

Detailed analysis contents include:

1. Localized data storage: Whether there is outbound and cross-border data transfer; Whether overseas personnel have read, write, download, delete and other permissions to the database storing personal data; etc.

2. Data collection, storage, usage, processing, transfer, provision, disclosure, deletion and other processes in the data life cycle: Whether personal data collection is legal; Whether the personal data subject is fully informed and consent; Whether the principle of minimum necessity is met; Whether personal sensitive data is de-identified, encrypted stored and transmitted; Whether the data beyond the retention period has been deleted and destroyed; Whether the personal data display is masked; etc.
3. Relevant internal management systems: Whether there is a delegated person in charge responsible for data security and protection; Whether a personal data protection mechanism has been established; Whether the data is protected and managed by classification; Whether the whole process data security management system has been established and improved; Whether there is relevant access management; Whether there is a complete personal information security impact assessment process; Whether the enterprise enter into a written cooperation agreement with the 3rd party institutions when entrust the 3rd party institution to handle personal data, etc.
4. Technical measures: Whether the cyber security level protection system is implemented; Whether there is a network partition; Whether there are technical measures to prevent computer viruses, network attacks, network intrusion and other acts endangering cyber security; Whether technical measures are taken to monitor and record network operation status and network security events, and relevant network logs are kept according to regulations; Whether there are real network attack and defense drills and safety emergency response drills; Whether there is real personal financial data in the non-production environment; Whether there is screen watermark; etc.
5. Personal data subject rights: Whether there is a process to support personal data subjects to view and copy their personal information; Whether there are corresponding processes and measures to support the withdrawal of personal data subjects from consent; Whether to provide data portable service to customers when they want to transfer their data to other service providers; etc.

The above examples are the dimensions that enterprises can refer to for gap analysis.

2.2 Step Two: Action Plan

When the compliance gap of the enterprise is determined, the most important thing is to have an action plan. When formulating the action plan, the enterprise should start from the actual behavior. The process is to know the current state of the enterprise, so as to know the distance from the ideal state, and formulate an action plan that can be implemented according to the gap analysis result. To formulate an action plan that can be implemented, the following aspects can be considered: Why, How, What, Who, When and Where.

Why
With the introduction of various laws and regulations, for enterprises, if they cannot ensure data security, they cannot ensure business security. With the increase of punishment by law, in addition to the enterprise itself, the relevant responsible persons may

also be punished. Criminal risk is more unbearable for enterprises, so the enterprise must draw a red line in the enterprise compliance system.

How

After analyzing the cross-border data transfer, data management life cycle, management system, technical means and personal data subject rights, the enterprise can find gaps. For example, one of the requirements from JR/T0171-2020 Personal Financial Information Protection Technical Specification is that real personal financial information cannot be used in non-production environment [4], then the technical measure is to anonymize the real personal data in the existing non production environment; From the perspective of management measures, it is necessary to formulate corresponding processes and define specific departments and operation steps to process personal financial data regularly imported from the production environments to non-production environments.

What

When the gap analysis is transformed into specific requirements, these requirements need to be classified and prioritized. For some problems, deficiencies, defects and requirements that have been reflected or can be expected, a scheme to solve the overall problem needs to be proposed, which is a list of actions with specific requirements, owners of tasks, deadline, progress status, etc. Examples are as follows (Table 1):

Table 1. Action plan example

Relevant regulations	Gap analysis	Category	Requirements	Owner	Deadline	Status
Implementing category/classification-based management of personal information	No data category/classification approach or category-based management mechanism	Process improvement	1. Set up Data Classification and Security Standards 2. Manage personal data in information systems based on Data Classification and Security Standards	Data Governance Senior Manager Lawyer Compliance Senior Manager	2021/11/01 2022/03/31	

Who

Different management measures or technical measures will involve different teams and personnel. For example, network partitioning requires colleagues in the infrastructure team; For data encrypted storage, the responsible parties are delivery teams. Sometimes it needs the cooperation of different departments. For example, data classification needs the data governance team and the legal compliance team to work together to decide the classification criteria, the data management specialists of the business teams classify the critical business data elements, and IT delivery teams should conduct security management on the information systems they manage according to the data classification.

When

Some gaps can be filled in a short time, such as appointing the person in charge of data protection and formulating personal data protection system and reasonable data authority management, etc. Some require enterprise level planning. For example, data encryption storage, network log retention period, etc. Different solutions take different time, and the implementation time of laws and regulations should be considered as well. Some laws may have a period around one month or two months from ratification to the effective date, but there is no grace period. Therefore, when making plans, the enterprise should fully consider the actual situation of resources and personnel, as well as the effective time of laws and regulations. The action plan should be completed before the law effective date.

Where

The gap analysis does not mean that all gaps can be closed in this Data and Cyber Security Improvement Program. At this time, the enterprise should decide where to spend time and resources through the dimension of risk acceptance. From the perspective of risk, there are some gaps with low risk. For example, due to business needs, the data on the information system used by internal employees needs to be in plain text and cannot be masked. Through risk assessment, because the risk can be reduced through reasonable and proper access control with additional control like screen watermark, then risk acceptance approach can be taken.

2.3 Step Three: Implementation

When the action plan has been prepared and prioritized, Data and Cyber Security Improvement Program could be implemented. Implementation is a process of project management with few steps. The key task is to set up a project formally.

Data compliance should take a top-down approach, so the involvement of senior executives is necessary. Gap analysis and action plan need to be supported and approved by senior executives. Therefore, one or more rounds of discussions are needed to finalize an action plan which is unanimously approved and adopted by all senior executives. After the action plan is approved, the implementation can be completed through the following steps:

1. Set up project team

The action plan may involve different departments or different teams in the same department. So, it is very necessary to identify key stakeholders, including proper project manager, business owners, business sponsors, responsible persons for different actions, people to be consulted and informed. In general, it is to use RACI (R = Responsible, A = Accountable, C = Consulted, I = Informed) model to list all key stakeholders together with relevant responsibilities. Let's take a requirement to set entrusted data processor management process as an example (Table 2).

Table 2. Example of RACI

	Data owner	Legal and compliance	IT delivery	IT security	IT risk	Data protection officer
Personal Data Ownership	A/R					
Put Privacy Policy on platforms	A	C	R	C	C	C
Data encryption transmission			R	A	C	
Assess the service capability and reliability		C	A/R	C	C	
Assess the security of information system				A/R	C	
Assess the data protection capability				A/R	C	C
Define the responsibilities and obligations in contract, etc.		C			A/R	C
Keep records of the handling of personal data by entrusted data processor	A/R					C
On-going monitoring of entrusted data processor					A/R	I

2. Define proper solutions

After the establishment of the project team, the Data and Cyber Security Improvement Program entered the planning stage. The project planning stage includes the determination of work tasks, task decomposition, priority arrangement, budget cost and risk management. A very important work here is to define proper solutions. Especially when it comes to the improvement of technical measures, a comprehensive solution is needed. There are many factors to consider in such a solution. Let's take the requirements for encrypted data storage as an example.

For the solution of data encryption, the method and usage scenario of data encryption should be considered.

For data-at-rest i.e., data in cloud storage or on prem, there are 4 levels in the increasing order of protection: Disk level, File system level, DB level and application level (Table 3).

For data-in-use i.e., data that is being used or processed in the public cloud or in applications on prem, the enterprise may implement confidential computing solutions if available. Confidential computing solutions protect data by isolating sensitive data in a protected, hardware based computing enclave during processing.

Table 3. Encryption methods and purpose

Encryption	Address for
Application level	Malicious direct database access
Database level	Malicious copy database files, not useful for authorized database users
File level	Malicious copy files, not useful for file system admin and authorized file users
Disk level	Disk physical loss

For data-in-transit i.e., data that traverses to and from, and within prem and the public cloud, the solution could be encryption protocol or application-level data encryption to mitigate the information disclosure risk during transit.

So, the overall encryption solution is as below (Table 4):

Table 4. Encryption solution

Data at rest	Data in use	Data in transit
1. For data need to be revertible, encryption should be used – Application level Database level File level Disk level	1. Masking – At Display layer, for sensitive data that do not need to be displayed in plain text	1. Traffic in internet – Encryption protocol must be used
2. Key management system should be dedicated with self-managed encryption key	2. For analysis data – Tokenize the personal identity information where possible	2. Traffic in intranet between office and Data Center (both on public cloud and on-prem); Traffic in intranet between public cloud and on-prem – Encryption protocol must be used, especially for customer data in the traffic without application-level encryption
		3. Traffic in intranet within Data Center – Encryption protocol should be used wherever possible

After defining the solution, perform task decomposition on the solution. Task decomposition is the WBS (Work Breakdown Structure) principle in project management: Decompose the solution according to certain principles and descend layer by layer. Each lower level represents a more detailed definition of the project work and decomposes the task until it can no longer be divided.

3. Project execution and monitoring

After the task is decomposed, the project is ready, and the implementation of the project should be started, which is project execution stage. In this stage, it is to start to assign specific tasks, confirm the start/end date and priority of each task, etc. In the project execution management, the most important thing is to do a good job in communication management. The effective communication between members is a series of measures to ensure the reasonable collection and transmission of project information. And at the same time, communication is to be done to key stakeholders and senior executives to give them updates about project status, main achievements and let the know what kind of support is needed.

Project monitoring should also start at the same time during the execution of the project. Monitoring the project work is to track, review and report the project progress, so as to ensure that each project implemented is in accordance with the established objectives, plans and timelines. It is the process of evaluate project performance and project objective achievement in the project management plan.

4. Close the project

When all solutions have been implemented and all tasks have been completed, close the project is the process of completing all project management activities to formally end the project or phase. At the end of the project, the project manager needs to review the closing information of previous stages to ensure that all project work has been completed.

At this time, make another evaluation to ensure that all the gaps have been closed or risk accepted. Keep all project materials as evidence of data compliance. The materials include but is not limited to:

Assessment object and scope

Assessment Result

Gaps and rectification measures

Solutions

Actions taken

Output and deliverables,

etc.

Data compliance is not a one-off task, or it could not be resolved in one project. That's why, the landing of data compliance need a program. And the 3 steps should be conducted as a circle (Chart 2).

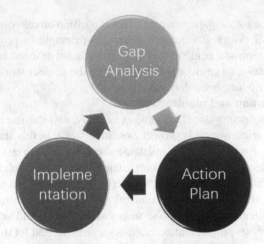

Chart 2. 3 steps circle for data compliance

References

1. Cyber Security Law of the People's Republic of China
2. Data Security Law of the People's Republic of China
3. Personal Information Protection Law of the People's Republic of China
4. JR/T0171-2020 Personal Financial Information Protection Technical Specification

On the 5G Edge Network Challenges of Providing Tactile and Multi-modality Communication Services

Tianji Jiang[1]([⊠]), Xiaonan Shi[2], Jiajin Gao[1], and Peng Liu[2]

[1] China Mobile Technologies (USA), Milpitas, CA, USA
{tianjijiang,jiajingao}@chinamobile.com
[2] Research Institute of CMCC, Ltd., Beijing, China
{shixiaonan,liupengyjy}@chinamobile.com

Abstract. Tactile & multi-modality communication, or TACMM, is a type of advanced interactive service that is currently being studied in the 3GPP 5G SA working groups. With the objective of achieving economical communication overhead, ultra-low latency, high reliability, and top security, it features multi-modal interactions among a group of service entities that are located in Telco's mobile edges. The benefits of seamlessly integrating multiple types of inputs sourced via multiple channels make it widely applicable in fields, like AR/VR, Telepresence, Immersive gaming, etc. TACMM generally consists of four modalities, namely, video, audio, ambient-sensor, and haptic detection. Depending on respective requirements and versatile data characteristics, they will unavoidably post challenges to the underlying communication networks, e.g., data sampling pattern, QoS differentiation, intra- and inter-modality synchronization, excessive datagram overhead, etc. In this paper, we present and analyze these different types of network challenges in 5G MEC environment upon providing TACMM services, from the perspective of Telco Operators, and then discuss potential schemes that could address them from different aspects as our future work.

Keywords: 5G & Edge · Multi-modality · Tactile · Time-sensitive network · QoS

1 Introduction

The rapid evolution, widespread adoption and extensive deployment of the 5G technologies have led to the prosperity of various advanced interactive services (AIS) that have been targeted for the 5G Edge deployment. The successful delivery of AIS at 5G Edge is extremely critical for mobile network operators (MNO's) since they have invested significantly in 5G networks and are seeking for effective ways to monetize their stakes. The 5G characteristics of RAN openness, network function virtualization, system disaggregation, control and user plane separation, and etc., all together provide numerous scenarios for the edge-service provisioning and deployment variations.

Tactile & multi-modality communication, or TACMM, is a type of advanced service that is currently being studied in the SDO 3GPP 5G SA working groups [1]. With

© Springer Nature Switzerland AG 2022
L.-J. Zhang (Ed.): EDGE 2021, LNCS 12990, pp. 85–92, 2022.
https://doi.org/10.1007/978-3-030-96504-4_7

the objective of achieving economical communication overhead, ultra-low latency, high reliability and top security, it features multi-modal interactions among a group of service entities that are distributed at the mobile network edges. The benefits of seamlessly integrating multiple types of inputs sourced via multiple channels make it widely applicable in fields, like industry manufacturing, robotics and telepresence, AR/VR, healthcare, gaming, education, etc. [2, 3].

Multi-modality communication service can both consolidate the inputs from more than one source and disseminate information to multiple destinations. This type of communication scheme possesses intrinsic advantages of providing services that would be complementary to each other, or even bearing progressive add-on gains, so that redundant delivery and information accuracy could be achieved effectively.

TACMM service in 5G, as shown in the following picture, can be generally categorized into four modalities, namely, video, audio, ambient-sensor and haptic detection, that would affect user experiences:

- Video: Can be still images, (on-demand) live images or interactive images.
- Audio: Voice data including human conversation, background noise, etc.
- Ambient-sensor: Process and transmit information as acquired in the field by various sensors, like brightness, temperature, humidity, smell, etc.;
- Haptic data: can be the feeling of touch, like the pressure, texture, vibration of medias, and the kinaesthetic senses, like the gravity, pull forces, position awareness, etc.

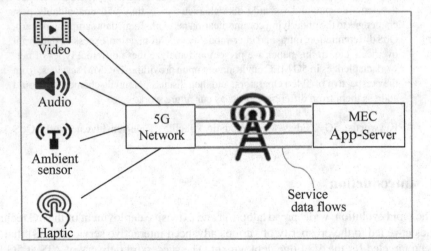

Individually, each modality forms a multi-stage closed-loop control that is comprised of remote information collection, data transmission, local processing and instruction feedback. Conjointly, four modalities could form an integrated system that requires to seamlessly synchronize the inter-modal information and make collective decision. Further, depending on the use cases, e.g., multi-person cloud gaming, the process could involve either point-to-point or point-to-multipoint group communications. Evidently, if both the intra- and inter-modality transmissions could be effectively handled and interpreted, then the communication will be more accurate, processing delay will be capped, feedback will be more agile, and the service will be of higher quality. The result is naturally better QoE, or quality of experience.

2 Challenges

In general, the 5G TACMM service requires adequately periodic, deterministic and reliable communication channels across modalities. Further, for some specific use cases, like remote surgery, online concert, etc., the requirement for achieving low latency is so high and for time drift is so tight that the processing and synchronization among multiple modalities would be best handled at edge locations, e.g., at Telco's mobile edges. From the perspective of a MNO, i.e., mobile network operator, the location could even be at far-edge which we will explain later.

Thanks to the unique nature and different requirements across modalities, and especially to address the 5G service requirements of different types of media steams with coordinated throughput, latency and reliability, TACMM faces challenges on various aspects, e.g. data characteristics, accurate synchronization, QoS differentiation, large volume of small packets, and packet-size variation, etc.

2.1 Characteristics of Generated Data Across Modalities

For example, according to the physiological perception, haptic data requires specific characteristics of frequency and latency in order to achieve 'acceptable' quality. The sampling rate of a haptic device for teleoperation systems may reach 1000 times per second, which, given that samples are typically transmitted individually, will hence generate a traffic stream with 1000 packets per second [4]. Comparably, the data sampling rate for video traffic is 60 or 90 frames per second, depending on the image resolution. Obviously, the high frequent transmission of packets by haptic devices, potentially for a large number of wireless devices over a certain distance, would be a great challenge for 5G system.

2.2 Multi-modality Data Synchronization

The synchronous requirements could be either among different modalities, like visual-haptic feedback process in industrial manufacturing, for which multiple data inputs demand to reach the distributed wireless devices at very immediate moment, or within a single modality, like multiple sensors acquiring and communicating data over the same ambient-sensor modality. In 5G system, the synchronization requires both high accuracy, which could reach sub-1 ms of time-sync, and large scalability, involving a large number of wireless devices (or UEs) possibly over a relatively large area. For example, in the scenario of sound field reappearing, different channels of sounds are sent to the distributed sound boxes to simulate the sound from a particular direction. A small time-deviation will cause significant direction error which will impact user experience severely. In some cases, the time difference of 1 ms may cause more than 30° angle error. Another scalable scenario is of multi-modality telepresence, for which tens of wireless devices require precise time synchronization for the transmission of control and visual signals.

2.3 Multi-modality QoS Differentiation

Each respective modality and the corresponding media stream have generally different QoS requirements over bandwidth, latency, jitter, loss, reliability, etc. For example, the communication latency (excluding data rendering and processing) for transferring audio-video frames should be less than 10 ms, while that for the haptic feedback & sensing is reasonably within 5 ms. The data reliability requirements for audio-video is normally 99.9%, for sensing information like user positioning & view is 99.99%, and for haptic feedback is 99.9% without compression or 99.999% with compression. The average data rate requirements across modalities are also different. For example, audio could be 5–512 Kbps, video 1–100 Mbps, sensing information ~1 Mbps, and haptic from 100 ~4K PPS depending on the usage of encoding compression.

2.4 High-Volume of Small-Size Packets, Along with Packet-Size Variations

As indicated in IEEE 1918.1 [3], the size of each haptic packet is related to the capacity of DoF, i.e., Degree of Freedom, that a haptic device may support. While the data size for one DoF is 2–8 Byte, a haptic device might support 6^+ DoFs. Depending on whether an encoding algorithm uses compression or not, the generated traffic volume of haptic modality may reach 1 K–4 K PPS (w/o haptic compression), or 100–500 PPS (with compression). For small-size packets with high PPS, the overhead of the header encapsulation as introduced by underlay networks, when coupled with the impact from additional reliable schemes, may severely degrade the transmission efficiency, or so-called good-throughput. Another potential challenge is the variation of packet sizes among different modalities. For example, in a typical TACMM use case, audio frame size is 50–100 Bytes, video frame size is 1 K–10 K Bytes, and haptic data frame is having 2–8 Bytes per DoF with 6^+ DoFs. Since there is no one-fit-all protocol, we might need to explore new technologies.

3 Address the Challenges

Nowadays, the study phase of the 3GPP 5G TACMM service is close to completion [1]. This phase mainly focuses on exploring typical edge scenarios that would cover as many practical use cases as possible. Following the study efforts is the common normative phase that will work on the detailed implementation standards. TACMM is an on-going effort with the delivery target for 3GPP 5G Rel-18 [5]. Since the standards are yet to be investigated, this section will only provide some reference thoughts that could potentially address the challenges from the network perspective. This is a brief discussion without diving into too many details, which are indeed our future work.

3.1 Distributed Edge-Computing Architecture

As we elucidated previously, the commonality to many use cases in TACMM service is the need for communication mechanism that could be characterized by extremely low latency, as well as the processing locality that would feature the timely handling of multi-sourced input data. For 5G mobile operators, these will naturally lead to the adoption of mobile edge-computing technologies.

Thanks to various factors like existing infrastructure buildup, diversified service offering, dynamic business justification, etc., a mobile network operator (MNO) cannot normally adopt the single edge-cloud architecture to accommodate both networking and non-networking services. Therefore, MNOs will generally build a distributed edge-cloud platform that is comprised of multiple building blocks, namely far-edge, aggregation-edge and edge clouds[1]. The following picture shows indeed a practical design and real field deployment case from a well-know MNO with global reach.

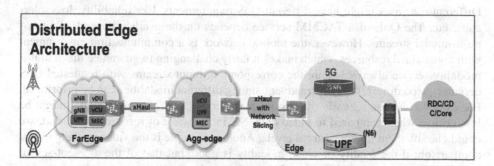

Under 5G context, for accommodating diversified requirements of multi-modal tactile services, the access network and 5G-UPF could be deployed in various locations. For example, some edge applications with multi-point deployment has low-latency and high-resolution synchronization requirement among modalities. Therefore, the UPF and the associated processing controller would be best positioned close to UEs, i.e., in the far-edge cloud as indicated in the above picture, for better supporting the coordination among data flows. Normally, the QoS specification among modalities are different. So, a virtualized CU (vCU) function could be deployed closer to cell-site such that the IP header of mobile traffic would be exposed earlier for differentiated QoS treatment among multi-modal steams.

3.2 Time Sync Mechanism

5G-UP is built over IP networks. The scalability requirement of underlying network makes a true challenge the time synchronization accuracy of TACMM service that could reach sub-1 ms. If the TACMM service is further provided by a 3rd-party provider but not the mobile operator (MNO) itself, then the synchronization would have to cross administrative domains. Fortunately, an MNO will normally have contracts with 3rd-party service providers that would make the collaborations more smoothly.

The IETF Deterministic Networking (DetNet) working group [6] collaborates with IEEE802.1 Time-Sensitive Networking (TSN) [7] to focus on deterministic data paths over both layer-2 and layer-3 networks. DetNet addresses the networks under the single administrative-control, which would make the intra-modality time-sync relatively

---

[1] Then, the connection beyond edge is further toward regional DC and core DC.

straightforward among participating entities. For inter-modality time-sync, [8] provides a potential scheme by introducing a reference stream for clock synchronization. Another approach that is being investigated in 3GPP is to have the receiving device compare the time stamps (of packets) and process the multiple streams accordingly. However, the approach faces the challenge that the sending time stamps (of packets) among different streams might not be synchronized, which would lead to potentially even greater misalignment at the destination.

3.3 Prioritized Treatment Among Different Modalities

Different use cases might have different QoS requirements, like reliability, loss tolerance, etc. The QoE of a TACMM service depends on the availability and quality of multi-modal streams. However, the mobile network is a communication environment with constrained resources, which makes it fairly challenging to guarantee that a multi-modality service always acquire the corresponding input streams with requested QoS demand. Accordingly, the QoS treatment among different modalities can be prioritized. For example, for the scenario of 'remote control robot' [1], the audio signal might be less critical when compared to video data. So, in the wake of resource constraint, we could classify them into prioritized levels. Another example is the video-sensing modal comparison; if the quality of video modality is good, but that of the ambient-sensor modality is experiencing difficulty, then, with coordination, some less critical sensing information like 'brightness' could be dropped since the 'visual signal' from the video modality can be a good substitution[2].

3.4 Prioritized Treatment Within a Modality

The prioritized QoS treatment can also be applied within a modality. For example, if the bandwidth of video modality is limited, then we could utilize the image encoding mechanism in MPEG [9], and, depending on the criticalness of I, P, and B frames, adopt a hierarchical scheme to prioritize the frame transmission [10][3]. I-frames might be given higher QoS preference when compared to P and B frames. In this, even if the restrained bandwidth on video modality might prevent wireless devices from getting the best-quality images, leading to in-modality service degradation, images with the basic quality can still be transmitted and rendered. This kind of controlled prioritization should be better than the random frame selection, transmission and dropping if congested. The similar consideration could be applied to the ambient-sensor modality to address the multi-sensor data generation with some sensor(s) being more critical in a use case.

---

[2] We want to point out that the standardization of the definition of multi-modality QoS is still an on-going work in 3GPP SA WG.

[3] We are aware that [10] focused on the IP multicast communication. Comparably, in 3GPP SA WG, the 5G MBS has just passed the study-phase, and is currently in the normative phase. There are lots of on-going MBS work in 5G system, which, once standardized, will integrate with the IP network domain, via a PDU session off the 5G-Core N6 interface, to provide end-to-end multicast service [12].

3.5 Small-Size Packets with Large Volume

The haptic modality in TACMM service will generate large volume of packets per second with small packet size. Upon transmission, the overhead of the header encapsulation as introduced by underlay networks, when coupled with the impact from additional reliable requirements, may severely degrade the transmission efficiency. QUIC is a transport layer network protocol initially designed, implemented, and deployed by Google. Nowadays, the IETF QUIC WG is working to standardize the protocol [11]. QUIC provides zero round-trip-time (RTT) connection establishment and transmission. This could potentially benefit the haptic data transmission. Another idea is to coalesce multiple small-size packets to spare the encapsulation overhead associated with individual small packets.

4 Conclusion

Tactile & multi-modality communication, or TACMM, is a type of advanced interactive service that is currently being explored in the SDO 3GPP 5G SA working groups. It strives to achieve ultra-low latency, high reliability, top security and low communication overhead. TACMM features normally four modalities, namely, video, audio, ambient-sensor and haptic detection. Depending on respective requirements and versatile data characteristics, there exist challenges to the underlying communication networks, e.g., characteristics of generated data, synchronization among/within modalities, QoS differentiation, handling of small-size datagrams, etc. In this paper, we present and analyze these challenges in 5G MEC environment, from the perspective of Telco Operators, and then discuss potential schemes that could address the TACMM service from different aspects.

Nowadays, the TACMM standardization process in 3GPP is still on-going [1, 5]. While closely monitoring its progress, we will be researching various challenges, based on the current operational status and the future planning of our company's 5G networks as well as the adoption of edge-computing technologies, as our future work.

References

1. 3GPP TR 22.847: Study on supporting tactile and multi-modality communication services
2. ITU-T Technology Watch Report: The Tactile Internet August 2014
3. Holland, O., et al.: The IEEE 1918.1 "Tactile Internet" standards working group and its standards. In: Proceedings of IEEE, vol. 107, no. 2 (2019)
4. Rank, M., et al.: Predictive communication quality control in haptic teleoperation with time delay and packet loss. IEEE Trans. Hum.-Mach. Syst. 46(4), 581–592 (2016)
5. 3GPP 5G SA Tdoc: S1-210086, Study on supporting tactile and multi-modality comunication services
6. Finn, N., et al.: Deterministic Networking Architecture, RFC 8655 (2019). https://www.rfc-editor.org/info/rfc8655
7. IEEE 802.1 Time-Sensitive Network Task Group. https://1.ieee802.org/tsn/
8. LI, Y., et al.: One-way Delay Measurement Based on Reference Delay, IETF-draft. https://datatracker.ietf.org/doc/draft-li-ippm-ref-delay-measurement/
9. Mitchell, J., et al.: MPEG Video Compression Standard, Chapman and Hall, Boston (1997)

10. McCanne, S., et al.: Receiver-driven layered multicast. ACM SIGCOMM Computer Communication Review (1996)
11. IETF QUIC Working Group. https://datatracker.ietf.org/wg/quic/about/
12. 3GPP TR 23.757, Study on architectural enhancements for 5G multicast-broadcast services

Author Index

Printed in the United States
by Baker & Taylor Publisher Services

Printed in the United States
by Baker & Taylor Publisher Services